Lessons in Lightness

THE ART OF EDUCATING THE HORSE

MARK RUSSELL

WITH ANDREA W. STEELE

Foreword by Bettina Drummond

THE LYONS PRESS
Guilford, Connecticut
An imprint of The Globe Pequot Press

Copyright © 2004 by Mark Russell and Andrea W. Steele

First Lyons Press paperback edition, 2007

The Lyons Press is an imprint of The Globe Pequot Press.

10 9 8 7 6 5 4 3 2 1

Printed in the United States of America

Designed by Maggie Peterson

Photographs by Ellen Leffingwell, Photography to Remember, unless otherwise noted.

Illustrations by Andrea W. Steele unless otherwise noted.

Page iv: Cecily L. Steele, *Half-Pass Trot*. This drawing of Nuno Oliveira and Ousado was inspired by a photograph in *Reflections on Equestrian Art*.

ISBN: 978-1-59921-071-1

The Library of Congress has previously cataloged an earlier (hardcover) edition as follows:

Library of Congress Cataloging-in-Publication Data

Russell, Mark, 1951 Nov. 13-
    Lessons in lightness : the art of educating the horse / Mark Russell with Andrea W. Steele ; foreword by Bettina Drummond.
            p. cm.
    ISBN 1-59228-360-8 (trade cloth)
                1. Horses—Training. I. Steele, Andrea W. II. Title.

        SF287.R87 2004
        636.1'0835—dc22

                                                    2004048769

The apex of perfection in equestrian art is not an exhibition of a great deal of different airs and movements by the same horse, but rather the conservation of the horse's enjoyment, suppleness and finesse during the performance. . . so moving is the sight of perfectly unisoned movements.

—Nuno Oliveira
Reflections on Equestrian Art

CONTENTS

The most interesting aspect of Nuno Oliveira's legacy to the riding community is the variety of interpretation that his philosophy, rather than his methodology, has spawned. As I read Mark Russell's words, they brought to mind our teacher's voice telling me that there is no actual definable technique; there is only the ability of each rider to find the right measure of tact to present the questions in such a way as to be acceptable to the individual needs of a particular horse.

In riding, as in all interpretative art forms, it is how the art is taught and transmitted by able communicators that is important, not how it is interpreted by the talent of an individual rider in presenting a visually pleasing or impressive package to draw new interest from outside eyes. In fact, it is the great sadness of this art that at the height of one's physical powers and at the cusp of the training levels, both rider and horse age beyond their peak and must rely on the memory of a feel and on the internal eye of the beholder to intuit what was once there. But, is this not how we feel our way around the first steps of our horses? To discern the potential movement, do we not have to "squint" to flesh out the conformation that is before us and, with our skill as trainers, breeders, or riders, fill in the next two years of work through our imagination? That the very last glance at the end of the training cycle depends on the very same criteria of judgment as at the beginning is perhaps the most fascinating and frustrating part of this art form.

To write about lightness, one must first reject seeing things from one's personal perspective. Imagine looking over a river to the far bank and seeing that far point, eagerly trying to guess what the real colors and textures of the vegetation growing there are like, what the feel of the earth, its density and smell, would be to your touch. You would be wondering if your feet would like to walk on that path, if your face would automatically reach up to the wind and sun in enjoyment of that space and moment. Well, that is what each rider is called upon to do by the horse that he is to learn from. The role of "teacher" within this craft is to throw a bridge across and to inspire others to have the boldness to place their feet on it, yet also to have the courage and trust to stand aside as they attempt to cross over.

Now, since one cannot teach long without going back to learning, imagine a suspension bridge lofted high over a smaller straight one, and this one in turn over a covered country one, and that one over a set of rudimentary planks, and you will see that the style of crossing and the capacity to reach over this flowing river of knowledge is all that differentiates one from the other, not the desire to reach this far bank called lightness.

As always, I am humbled by those teachers who have the desire to place in word form those engineering plans that they have experimented with in order to help others who might not have the opportunity to experience this form of educated construction. Books such as *Lessons in Lightness* bridge a variety of worlds and bring forth dialogues not merely between rider and horse but also traveler to traveler and, as such, become an invitation to stop for a moment and watch as another's journey takes on a recognizable form.

For those who do not have the opportunity to visit many countries, see masters at work, and spend countless hours watching them patiently building up horses, reforming bad shapes and awkward thinking processes, or transforming poorly formed muscle structures, such books are a necessary form of education and a generous sharing of all the risks, joys, and fears that define the individual rider. Regardless of the endless variables that create division and polemic among the various disciplines of training horses, each training endeavor must contain one essential ingredient: truth. Why do we cleave to these marvelous beings called horses? Because their instinct calls that truth out of us, just as the quality in the depth of their eyes calls out for an emotional response that sometimes defies our logic, self-preservation, and skill.

The truth belonging to Mark Russell has been long in forming, and I hope it will enable many other riders to seek out their own. From my perspective, up on the bridge that is my own bright and particular quest, I have stopped to watch him build with these words and have found that many of them form the same mortar that helped me build my ideas. As I continue forward, I am comforted that even if the look, shape, and feel of training differs with each interpretation, we are all heading towards that one bank, across that same river.

Bettina Drummond
Pruyn Stud
Washington, Connecticut

Twenty years ago my view of horsemanship changed, and, like a reve-lation, it happened almost instantly. On that day, I watched a remark-able horse and rider demonstrate a partnership that transcended everything I understood about the boundaries between horse and master—this horse and rider appeared to communicate as equals. The desire to achieve such exquisite union led me on a lifelong quest and turned the sport I loved into art.

— — ·•· — —

I began riding and training Western performance horses in my teens. In those early years I often saw my training efforts hampered by the limitations of poorly shod horses. Guided by the old saying "If you want something done right, do it yourself," I enrolled in farrier school and learned to shoe.

By the late 1970s my business was split equally between shoeing and training. The fact that I was shoeing most of the horses I trained gave me a personal perspective into the unique way each horse trav-eled. It allowed me to feel from the saddle the effects of any corrective measures I'd made to the hoof. As my client list grew, I gained exposure to other riding disciplines outside the Western sphere. An introduction to dressage inspired me to examine the origins of classical horseman-ship and the writings of the "old masters." As a result I came to view dressage as essential to all horse training and incorporated its funda-mental exercises into my own program regardless of riding discipline.

In the 1980s, while pleased with my success in horse training and the direction of my career overall, I wasn't content. There was an ever-present sense that something was absent from my work, some secret yet to be discovered. When a client invited me to attend a clinic with the Portuguese trainer Nuno Oliveira (1925–1989), who was touring the United States at the time, I agreed to join her though I had no particular knowledge of Oliveira or his work. The moment I saw Master Oliveira ride, I knew the secret that had eluded me was right before my eyes. I saw not only lightness, balance, and harmony, but a horse that was happy and proud in his work. Oliveira's humanity spoke to me through the movement of his horse—this was my revelation.

I stayed at that clinic for three days. Later, traveling to Portugal, I spent time as an observer at Oliveira's school. While there, my perception of horse training changed dramatically: All of what I knew about the process collided with Oliveira's way of interpreting the horse. Through Master Oliveira's instruction, I learned the principles of riding in lightness, principles that had their roots in the teachings of the old masters, methods now referred to as classical dressage. In my lessons I learned to feel the horse as never before. That was Master Oliveira's gift to me. He taught me to learn from the horse every single day, to listen to the horse, and to feel from the horse—on the horse's terms, not mine. He taught me to focus on the nuances of communication, nuances that had escaped me in the past. I came away from that experience with a deep sense of understanding and purpose.

Since then I've worked with students and horses of all abilities and every background. Training in lightness gives the rider insight into an educational process whose goal is to achieve optimal unity between horse and rider. No matter how well you ride or how talented your horse may be, he can only do what you prepare him for and then ask for correctly. That is why a successful training program must work horse and rider together as a unit.

Horses, like my students, try to please. I haven't ridden many horses that are bad by nature. Given their innate willingness to oblige, it is our responsibility as riders to learn all we can and never take unjust advantage of their good nature.

I wrote this book about my methods and my program because riding in lightness works for both the horse and the rider. Few trainers, however, have carried the classical knowledge of lightness forward. In my own work I often see flagrant misunderstandings between horse and rider, yet I find most riders—and horses—willing and able to improve. To understand how the horse thinks and how he creates forward impulsion and propels energy through his body empowers the rider to better educate the horse. An exploration into the horse's physiological and psychological state is the basis for building that strong bond most riders yearn for. Learning lightness opens the door to the art of riding.

Mark Russell and Yoda. Photo: Andrew Forbes

In essence this book describes a system that gives the rider the knowledge to educate the horse so that he becomes a better horse to ride. It shows how to develop the horse gymnastically, so he can respond correctly to the aids. This step-by-step program also teaches the rider to learn from the horse just as I did twenty years ago. Please join me on an adventure into what is truly an art—the art of educating the horse, for this is where it all begins. At the end of the journey, if you find that teaching the concepts of lightness to the horse allows you to ride and interact with the horse on a deeper level, then this project has all been worthwhile.

ACKNOWLEDGMENTS

Throughout this project we have been deeply moved by the generosity and support of our friends and colleagues. We extend our gratitude to the following people who lent their time, knowledge, and skill to the project: Kevin Bayusik; Chip Beckett, DVM; Lawrence Brooks, DVM; Carol Cross of Kachina East Farm; Donald Brown; Nancy and John Esposito of Hidden Meadow Farm; Andrew Forbes; Amy Harris; Hela Koiv; Carl Lombard; Candice and Ted McNaughton of Rim Rock Farm; Joann Neils; Stanley Prymas; Deb Purdell; Debra Smith; Michael Steele; and Willis Steele. Thank you for grooming horses for photo shoots, or reading drafts of the text, or allowing us to use your property and equipment.

We are further indebted to Bettina Drummond whose lifelong commitment to riding in lightness is expressed in the foreword; Ellen Leffingwell who undertook the crucial task of photographing the horses; Cecily Steele for capturing the essence of lightness in her illustrations; and Gillian Belnap and Laura Strom of The Globe Pequot Press who skillfully guided us through the publication process. Your enlightened interest has been inspirational.

—Mark Russell and Andrea Steele

CHAPTER 1

Understanding Lightness

As riders, we are also teachers. We teach the horse every time we handle him. We either teach good things or bad things . . . it's all up to us.

By nature all horses are capable of true or pure movement. Yearlings of any breed can be seen performing passage across an open field on a blustery winter day. This is not taught—all horses are capable of range of motion within their gaits. While not necessarily ideal, it is uncompressed and true to that horse's natural gait. Because the horse is innately knowledgeable and capable of the exact movements we aspire to train, then as riders we must come to the training process with the commitment that we will maintain that trueness throughout all we do.

My theories and concepts are drawn from the teachings of the French and Iberian *écuyers,* or riding masters. They used suppling and gymnastic exercises to balance the horse in lightness. By using these methods the rider unleashes the horse's true movement without either driving force (the rider's legs) or holding restraints (the rider's hands). When the rider enables the horse to use his energy efficiently, the horse will drive himself forward; once balanced in self-carriage, there will be no resistance in the rein.

Riders of any discipline need to understand that each horse enters training with his own perception of balance and his own areas of stiffness that block energy flow within his body. When left to his natural instincts, the horse will resist or evade the rider's aids whenever he encounters stiffness or difficulty moving his body in the requested way.

In most cases this evasion is the horse's attempt to conform with what he believes the rider wants him to do, only in a way that is easier for him to accomplish. Riding in lightness teaches the horse to use his body in new ways, thereby changing his understanding of balance.

By suppling and strengthening the horse's entire body, tension and stiffness can be lessened, thus reducing resistance to the aids. With the release of tension and a lessening of stiffness, the rider can enhance the horse's true and natural gait as his balance becomes more educated. Ideally, this change in balance will develop as a package with the horse and rider working in unison. As the masters taught, the achievement of unison with lightness to the aids comes through relaxation.

Trueness of movement and relaxation are intrinsically linked: To maintain the softness of relaxation, the horse must stay within his realm of true movement. The training process should result in an enhanced gait, not one whose fundamental structure has been changed.

Relaxation allows the horse to stretch and become more flexible in his joints and muscles. In this supple state the rider can better align the horse's spine and optimize his length bend (see Key Terms), allowing him to obtain deeper engagement through flexion. This engaged position develops the necessary "carrying" muscles along the horse's back, which in turn allows the horse to transfer his center of gravity from the forehand to the area beneath the rider and ultimately obtain self-carriage, or equilibrium. Once the horse releases stiffness and tension throughout his body, there will be no resistance to energy traveling forward from the haunch. The horse then finds forward impulsion less of an effort.

Lightness develops through specific sequential steps: Relaxation and suppling exercises teach the horse to become highly efficient with energy flow. Simultaneously, the exercises develop the horse's gymnastic strength. By enhancing strength, the horse can more easily maintain balance. Once he has achieved self-carriage, the horse can stay light to all the aids.

Achieving lightness to the aids evolved from the School of Versailles and the philosophy of the French *écuyer* François Robichon de la Guérinière (1688–1751), which was later grafted onto the work of François Baucher (1796–1873). They are credited with being the first to promote the benefits of suppleness and flexion in the horse in order to achieve lightness. These concepts continued to be developed by trainers on the Iberian Peninsula and have come to be recognized as the artistic school of riding, or academic equitation.

Over the years, and most notably since the mid-twentieth century, the concept that relaxation be paramount in all training has been obscured by the dominance of a more precision-based style of training. This "competitive school" has affected more than dressage riding—its influences have been felt across the broad spectrum of horse training and competition.

Although postulating the same objectives of producing a supple, obedient horse with the strength to move in self-carriage, the competitive school uses methods very different from the artistic school for achieving these goals. Although the horse supples, flexes, and learns to balance through many of the same exercises discussed in this book, the competitive approach instructs the rider to drive forward with the leg and seat, then hold through the rein in order to achieve contact.

The competitive school rider actively uses the leg, seat, and hand in the horse's gymnasticing process. With less emphasis on and a different perception of relaxation, an impressive movement may be demonstrated sooner using these methods rather than by pursuing lightness. The end result may look similar, albeit poles apart to ride. The sequence in which suppleness, flexibility, and balance is achieved differs dramatically between these different schools of thought. While the beginning phase of training lightness can take time, the horse learns rapidly once there is an understanding of how to move in relaxation. In the end, however, there should be little difference in the overall training time between the two methods.

With the recent rise in popularity of what is now called natural horsemanship, many trainers are reintroducing the benefits of relaxation into their programs. While natural horsemanship does not equate to riding in lightness, there are conceptual similarities, most notably in the way the rider interacts and communicates with the horse. This much-sought-after connection has sparked new interest in relaxation as a training tool and, consequently, how to obtain lightness to the aids.

Modern masters, such as the late Nuno Oliveira in Portugal, never strayed far from the theories of Guérinière or Baucher. Master Oliveira practiced and taught a similar method of riding to a small but dedicated following whose foremost goal was lightness to the aids.

In the preface I mentioned the great privilege I had to learn from Master Oliveira. The system described in this book, while not strictly conforming to his teachings, certainly adheres to the spirit of the academic principals of using relaxation to obtain flexibility and strength. I have incorporated my own experiences into this training program in order to reach and appeal to a contemporary audience.

Lightness is not an alternative approach. Nor is it a "style" or a clinician's way to deliver fast results. This book describes methods that have stood the test of time, albeit different from what is considered mainstream by today's competition-based performance trainers.

Using these methods to facilitate the horse's initial shift in balance, creating what is called "a working frame," helps riders to understand more about the horse and his movement. A specific order of teaching the exercises develops the horse's new balance and frame while gaining lightness to the aids. Analyzing each exercise on a psychological and physiological level gives the rider insight into the very nature of the horse—insight into how he thinks and uses his body. As a result new channels of communication are opened. Lightness to the aids results in an intense and sensitive bond between horse and rider—it is that bond that elevates riding to an art.

Building or tuning the horse's body to correctly respond to the aids is the technical side of the program. The exercises that follow show how to prepare the horse to relax physically and mentally, releasing tension from his body and enabling him to respond to the slightest touch. The process of relaxing the horse and discovering lightness while advancing through the exercises takes time. Faith in the theory must exist. Some commonly used training techniques won't work under this system, not because other techniques are wrong, but because this system requires the rider to think about the process in different ways.

Riding in lightness challenges the rider to train without creating false movement, even temporarily. False movement is anything untrue for the individual horse or at a particular level of training. For example, most riders want the horse to have an almost vertical head carriage. If the horse's reluctance to bring or hold the nose in is viewed as the problem in and of itself, the solution can be narrow in scope. Many riders attempt to obtain a vertical head carriage by driving the horse forcefully into the hand or possibly using draw reins (or similar apparatus) to hold the position, thus risking false movement.

Achieving lightness to the aids means understanding that the horse moves as a whole and that for every action there is a reaction.

Restraining the head in any way creates tension and creates false movement. If the horse's head is forced into a visually appealing position, something else will give in the process. The horse may stiffen, drop his back, or exhibit any number of counterreactions. When training in lightness, the horse's head will flex once he has been gymnasticized (relaxed, suppled, and strengthened) and balanced to support flexion. Forcing the horse into any frame before he is ready risks a false foundation. No matter what is taught thereafter, true and balanced movement will be difficult to achieve. Forcing is not training; the rider need not become an adversary. The horse and rider should always be partners.

That's not to say there is no role for apparatus to assist in the training process. Even the old masters used draw reins under certain conditions. (Specific examples of appropriate uses are described in Longeing and in Tack

When the horse is relaxed, suppled, strengthened, and balanced in true movement, he can excel in any discipline for which he is suited.

and Accessories.) However, riders should understand the progression and priorities of each stage of training. Problems result when riders look for quick fixes. This often creates another problem or masks serious long-term issues.

The exercises presented here will explain how the rider/trainer teaches the horse to work in the best possible frame by being balanced, not by being restrained. The rider develops the horse gymnastically to facilitate relaxation, create flexibility, and build strength in all the forward gaits, rein-back, and lateral exercises. The true and balanced movement that is the result will carry forward into all the horse does.

Once the basics are accomplished, the horse can go on to learn advanced movements unique to any particular discipline. It really doesn't matter if those specifics are for more dressage work, Western riding, or jumping. When the horse is relaxed, suppled, strengthened, and balanced in true movement, he can excel in any discipline for which he is suited.

Building the basics is essential for any worthwhile endeavor, but this doesn't happen overnight. Riders should commit to an ultimate goal, so time becomes less of a factor in measuring success. Each horse and rider will advance at differing rates. What takes one team one week may take another team months. It is best to consider each ride part of an ongoing training program where small successes accumulate, producing better and better sessions over time.

Not all riders will choose to utilize every exercise offered in these pages. To ask that every ride be considered part of an ongoing program doesn't mean always aspiring to an ever-higher level. It can simply mean being competent and feeling good about riding—at any level.

Both riders and horses have limits. Due to injury or conformation faults, some horses may not be able to accomplish all the movements, though gymnastic exercises can improve agility and increase strength far beyond initial expectations. This system accepts limitations of both horse and rider.

Lessons in Lightness is about the art of developing the horse through an understanding of the complexities of how the horse thinks

Lightness to the aids results in an intense and sensitive bond between horse and rider.

and moves, so that the horse learns to respond rather than react. This is done for the sake of the horse and for the sake of the sport. Attention to the nuances of communication will greatly increase the likelihood that a strong emotional connection will develop between horse and rider.

I hope my explanation of the concepts and my description of the exercises will encourage riders to use this very practical program. I encourage everyone to stay the course and have patience for the remarkable results to come.

CHAPTER 2

Meet the Horses/ How to Use This Book

Educating the horse is like doing a jigsaw puzzle. The complete picture will only appear when all the pieces are in place.

This training system crosses riding disciplines and is appropriate for a wide variety of horses. While the specific rein aids require the use of a snaffle bit, virtually all types of saddles and bridles, either English or Western, are suitable. Proper fit to both horse and rider is the only prerequisite. Information regarding tack and related equipment is given in Tack and Accessories. Further, the training techniques are geared toward horses with prior experience under saddle. While the particular style of riding is not a concern, horses that have been badly handled may require a period of rehabilitation before responding to lightness.

MEET THE HORSES

The horses that demonstrate the exercises in this book were chosen because we believe that an "everyday" horse best represents the horse most of us own and train.

FANNY is a thirteen-year-old Thoroughbred mare. She sustained a shoulder injury at the track, which ended her racing career and jeopardized her longevity as a riding

horse. In fact, years of training attempts continually relapsed her into unsoundness. Once we started Fanny in this program, working in relaxation has helped her remain sound.

YODA is a thirteen-year-old Quarter Horse gelding. This horse's thought process is so intense that his ears are typically positioned as in the photo, awaiting instruction from the rider.

Yoda is a school master, teaching riders lightness through his response to the aids. He is equally competent under either English or Western tack.

EASTER is a seven-year-old Quarter Horse mare. Unbroken at age six, she has advanced to Phase II training in just seven months.

HOW TO USE THIS BOOK

For purposes of clarity, we refer to the horse as *he* and the rider as *she*. When discussing specific instructions for in-hand work, the term *trainer* (also *she*) is used to emphasize that the particular discussion is in hand and not mounted.

To best describe some exercises, the standard letter markers are used to designate the horse's position, movement, and/or direction within the manège.

This book describes a training system that asks the reader to develop an understanding of the concepts underlying riding in lightness. Success in the program lies as much in the acceptance of these concepts as in the application of the hands-on training techniques.

In explaining the concepts of lightness, comparisons with other training methods are sometimes useful. These methods are referenced here without criticism but as acknowledgment of the differences in techniques to achieve similar goals. Riders are advised to choose a training philosophy that best suits their own goals, then remain true to the teachings of that system.

Within the constraints of a book, the sequence and scope of each discussion is determined in advance. In practice, the individuality of each horse and rider may require minor changes in the teaching techniques or order in which lessons are taught. Our intention is to give the reader a thorough understanding of the concepts of riding in lightness along with a practical program for applying those concepts.

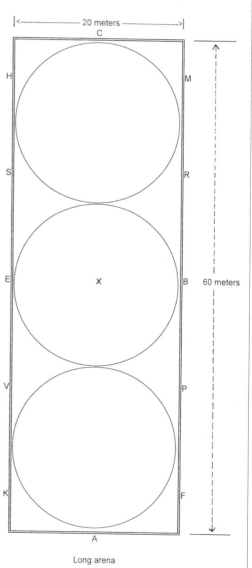

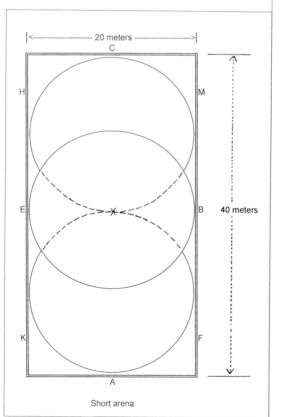

Standard-size riding arenas with letter markers.

CHAPTER 3

Teaching Lightness

*The horse is a herd animal that seeks a leader. To truly be a team,
the horse must accept the trainer as the leader. The trainer builds
this relationship through trust, kindness, friendship, and respect.*

The principal reason for teaching the horse to be light to the aids is
to create the healthy flow of energy through the horse's body. This
is achieved through relaxation. In teaching relaxation to the horse, the
trainer, in effect, offers the horse an *understanding* of how to let go and
release tension. The horse's thought process is as important as the
teacher's; in fact, the more the trainer recognizes the necessity for the
horse to understand, the better a teacher she will become.

Relaxation of the horse facilitates flexion, which provides the foundation for building the strength needed to achieve an educated, or academic, balance. Every detail of this training program relates to this
concept in some form. The exercises that follow progressively increase
the horse's degree of relaxation, flexion, and strength. When the horse
doesn't perform as expected, he either lacks the understanding or lacks
the relaxation, the flexion, or the strength to be correct. This thought
should be in the trainer/rider's mind during every schooling session.

Teaching lightness to the aids isn't difficult once the trainer/rider
understands how to move the horse forward in ways that efficiently use
his energy. The process of teaching the horse to coordinate and drive energy forward entails achieving relaxation and flexibility from front to
back so that the impulsion from the haunch can flow forward freely.

In teaching lightness, relaxation and flexion are introduced at the
front of the horse (the brain end) and continue to be offered through the

neck, along the back, across the pelvis, and down through the haunch and hind leg (the motor end). The energy produced from the haunch can then flow freely forward through the body, ultimately allowing the horse to be ridden from back to front in the most effective manner. This approach is circular in nature and needs to be recognized as an important element of teaching lightness. If the trainer/rider asks the horse to move forward from the haunch when there is tension or stiffness within his body, the muscles along the spine will absorb or block some of the forward motion. As a result, energy leaving the haunch will not reach the shoulders with the same strength. For example, feeling a lack of impulsion, many riders apply more leg to energize the horse. Driving the horse harder, however, does nothing to correct the resistance within the body. In short, both horse and rider try harder but get less. This is a significant source of frustration for many trainers/riders and horses.

This book offers trainers/riders an introduction to the movement of energy within the horse's body. By learning about each exercise and the parts of the horse's body each exercise addresses, the trainer/rider can supple the horse to move effectively. In the example above, using more leg to drive the horse harder *can* work, but achieving an understanding of why the horse stiffened will better serve the trainer/ rider—and the horse. By releasing tension the horse moves energy with greater ease, making forward impulsion less demanding on both horse and rider.

Although lightness is obtained through the relaxation of the horse, this assumes that the rider is also relaxed. The rider must release her own tension entirely in order to move in unison with the horse. Less reliance on the rein and the leg increases the horse's need to trust the meaning of the rider's subtle movements. In teaching lightness, rider self-awareness is a high priority. Correspondingly, the academic rider also needs to learn to interpret what the horse communicates through his body. Thus the rider learns from the horse just as the horse learns from the rider. This two-way process enables a strong bond to develop between horse and rider.

RELAXATION

Lightness is based on the three fundamentals of relaxation, flexion, and strength. Relaxation is the first step. Relaxation means teaching the horse to let go of stress and tension in his mind, and, hence, his body. Psychological relaxation leads to physical relaxation, which allows contracted muscles to return to their natural length. Relaxation is what lets the horse respond rather than simply react. A reaction is a reflex and, in animals, is most often based on instincts of self-preservation. Responding, in contrast, requires a thought process; it is the result of education. The trainer/rider offers the aid, allowing the horse to learn the desired response.

The horse is most likely to respond correctly if the trainer has taught him to relax and release tension in each part of his body. When the trainer has prepared the horse to move in a certain way and there is no physical resistance, or tension, within his body to interfere with the movement, he can *respond* to the aid in the intended way. Conversely, when unrelaxed, the horse is more likely to encounter resistance within his body and *react* instinctively rather than move through this tension.

To repeat, relaxation of the horse starts at the front. The jaw is the key that unlocks the body and opens the mind to accept relaxation. Loosening the jaw encourages the horse to lift and savor the bit in his mouth. Relaxing the jaw releases tension in the poll, encouraging the neck to lengthen down, thereby stretching the entire top line. The stretching process is the first step toward relaxation: It

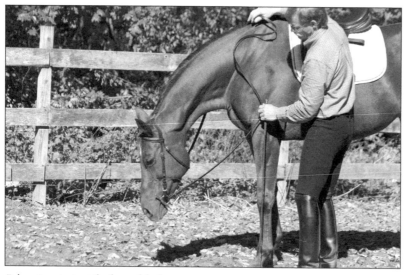

Relaxation starts at the front of the horse.

improves intramuscular blood flow and flexibility and prepares the muscles for strength development.

Gently vibrating the rein teaches the horse to relax the jaw (see Working In Hand). Once the horse relaxes his jaw, stretching his head and neck down delivers softness to the body. Lowering the head, even in a standing position, relaxes the horse's entire spinal column and begins the suppling process. Under saddle, this is often described as "nose to the ground." Starting as an exercise in hand, without the weight of the rider on his back, allows the horse to relax more easily. Recognizing softness and acknowledging a response begins the bonding process between horse and trainer/rider.

FLEXION

The second fundamental of lightness is flexion (see Key Terms). The horse must be limber throughout his body in order for energy to travel forward freely. Lateral and longitudinal exercises will develop his overall suppleness. Bending the length of the horse to the arc of a circle promotes side-to-side flexibility. Raising or rounding the back (in conjunction with the lowering of the hip) creates longitudinal bend.

Flexibility alleviates any resistance, or energy blocks, within the horse's body. The release of tension through stretching exercises is what allows the rider to move the horse freely. These exercises teach the horse which aids move which parts of the body (see Working In Hand and Phase II: Lateral Work Under Saddle). Well-defined aids open communication between horse and trainer/rider, thereby minimizing misunderstandings. By following the trainer/rider's precise instructions, the horse learns to relax and release inner tension at the exact point where resistance exists. The horse thus learns that the aids have a positive effect.

Sometimes the process of releasing tension will be easy—at other times it will be quite difficult. The same horse may release in some areas and not in others. This process can be complex and time-consuming. Trainers/riders are advised not to rush through the elementary exercises believing that the horse's suppleness will improve over time with higher-level movements. While this can happen, lightness takes a decidedly different approach: Always assess the horse by

Relaxation allows for maximum flexibility.

his current level of relaxation, flexibility, and strength. These are the terms on which the horse speaks to the rider. Advancement takes place only when the body complies easily with each task.

Some horses will remain flexible over long periods of time without any special suppling, while others will need to release tension at the start of each ride. The tension and stiffness that create energy blocks can be physical or psychological in nature; riders will have to deal with all aspects of what makes a particular horse who he is.

Patience in the initial phase of training pays great rewards. Relaxation allows for the freedom of movement—a tense horse will simply not be as flexible as a relaxed horse. By overlooking problems early on, the horse may advance before becoming technically correct in the movement. Since it is very difficult to return and solve problems after the horse learns to deviate or evade correct delivery, the trainer/rider is strongly cautioned not to train in a hasty, unaware manner. Ideally, the horse should achieve technical correctness while learning each exercise. If the horse is stiff, and a medical problem can be ruled out, the rigidity is his lack of relaxation. The degree of relaxation increases with greater flexibility and strength; however, the horse's accomplishment of each basic exercise should be relaxed to some degree and correct from the beginning.

Length bend. Easter shows a nice release in the novice position. She is giving to the inside rein while taking the outside rein down. Her relaxation is evident as she arcs her body to walk the curved line of a circle.

How the horse becomes flexible can be misunderstood. For instance, many riders overbend the horse thinking that this creates more softness. In reality it is counterproductive to ask the horse to bend in any way that is too deep. It only encourages false movement that will most likely be stiff and rigid. By teaching relaxation and

Longitudinal bend. Still in a novice position, Easter demonstrates relaxation through her top line.

stretching first, the horse becomes receptive to softening, flexing, and bending. This allows his movement to be true to his natural gait.

Flexing and suppling exercises are developed on circles and continue through a variety of lateral movements. Being forward on the circle creates length bend. Moving away from the bend in shoulders-in and counter-shoulders-in focuses on flexing first the haunch and then the shoulder. Finally, moving into the bend with half-pass, travers, and renvers produces the maximum degree of flexion and engagement. These gymnasticizing movements give the horse the tools to supple and release tension in specific areas of his body while learning the aids to move each part of his body, either independently or together. Riders of all disciplines need to understand the value of lateral work; it is not reserved for the dressage horse alone. The basic lateral movements will allow the horse to master any advanced performance, whether it be a 360-degree spin in a reining pattern or maneuvering rapidly with agility and control between fences on a show jumping course.

The gymnasticizing process, while technical in nature, is largely an art. The trainer/rider seeks to eliminate all resistances within the horse to achieve pure and true movement. However, seeking means just that—pursuing or striving to accomplish. In practice horse and rider will never attain zero resistance—each horse and rider will bring some misconception or physical shortcoming to the training process. Yet, in applying the aids to supple the horse, something wonderful occurs: Resistance gives way to relaxation and prepares the horse for the pursuit of lightness.

STRENGTH

The third fundamental for achieving lightness is strength. As the horse learns to relax and flex the spine through suppling exercises, those same exercises serve to build his body for stronger engagement. The added strength gives the horse the ability to create and carry forward movement with full impulsion.

Impulsion created through relaxation and flexion means that energy flows freely forward from the haunch, up through the back, through the withers, and ultimately through the horse's whole body. When the horse attains such efficient use of energy—by virtue of having no energy blocks within his body—his balance changes, and he begins to feel comfortable with his balance beneath the rider. The freedom of movement that is the result is true, or pure, and is what establishes the feeling of lightness to the rider. Building the horse's strength is essential to maintaining relaxation and achieving maximum lightness.

During the strength-building process, it is very important that the horse's spine is properly aligned through correct lateral and longitudinal bend. The initial step toward strong engagement is lengthening the horse down. This allows the haunch to move freely and step deeply underneath the body. True, it is the rider who asks for energy from the hindquarters, but it is what the horse does with the energy that is important. When energy flows forward through a properly aligned spine, the haunch carries the horse's weight, thereby building strength and useful impulsion. As the horse develops enough strength to carry and balance the impulsion beneath the rider, collection occurs with lightness through the hand and all the aids. At this point the horse is soft and flexible from front to back, enabling the rider to ride effectively from back to front.

Strength-building through rein-back.

CHAPTER 4

The Three Phases of Training

At each point in training, the rider needs to assess how much the horse understands and what he is physically able to perform. She does this by learning to listen to his body during every ride.

PHASE I TRAINING

The first stage of training concentrates on teaching the horse to relax and stretch. The rider encourages the horse freely forward without interference. In beginning Phase I, speed and rhythm are not so important as long as safety is maintained. Instead, the emphasis is on moving the horse freely forward such that, when stretched into a long-and-low position, his hind legs track well underneath his body.

Some horses will find freedom from the rider's direction confusing. Rushing is often an initial reaction. Don't pull the rein to slow the horse; instead, spiral inward on the circle—this requires the horse to slow himself down (see Phase I: Beginning the Circle). It is important that the horse never learns to hang on the bit or be supported by the rein in any way, just as it is important that the rider learns not to pull on the rein. This independence places the responsibility of balance on the horse, wherever his center of balance may be at that time. The training process will shift his center of balance to a point where he balances comfortably and consistently beneath the rider. Each exercise works progressively toward that goal.

Freedom to move forward and freedom from the rein also empowers the horse to think and make decisions. Quite often a green horse has surplus energy that he can't yet funnel into a lesson or otherwise control. Teaching the horse to relax is more productive than trying to

Easter is in the Phase I long-and-low frame. In this position of relaxation and slight length bend, the spine releases.

The horse's energy level and how he utilizes energy is discussed in Phase II: Building a Working Frame. Just remember that when you ride to tire the horse, you also condition him. Next time out, you will need to do even more. Once the horse is tired, the opportunity to teach is limited. This conditioning process does little or nothing to relieve the horse's inner tension or dissipate energy blocks within his body. A fundamental requirement of this system is to relax the horse so he can channel excess energy into a gymnastic exercise.

exhaust his energy. The tools for initiating relaxation are releases in hand, circles, and lateral movements.

As the horse stretches and supples laterally, his body begins to assume an "educated" form. Suppling into length bend and the corresponding engagement is at first strenuous. Excess energy is quickly dissipated through these exercises. As the horse's training progresses and his energy is better utilized, it can be channeled into developing scope in each movement.

Let's look at how the horse develops during Phase I:
- Relaxing and releasing the jaw allows the horse to relax into the bit and flex at the occipital poll.
- Lengthening the horse down into the lower position stretches the spinal column. This position releases tension in the muscles and joints, thereby facilitating relaxation throughout the horse's body.
- Moving in a long-and-low frame without contact in the rein encourages the horse to move forward freely and track deeply with his hind legs.

- Spinal alignment in the lower position asks the novice horse to follow his nose and bend around the rider's inside leg.
- Work on circles produces suppleness, improves spinal alignment, and initiates engagement.
- Spiraling to increase and decrease the size of the circle relaxes the horse's neck and body while flexing the spine in differing degrees of bend.
- Using the reins, either independently or together, to lead or support the bend teaches the horse to keep his shoulders level.
- Riding precise circles on the aids teaches the horse to move forward with length bend. This causes the inside hind leg to track into a position that increases engagement.
- With increased engagement, the front end lightens (albeit slightly), and the rider can begin to adjust the shoulders.

PHASE II TRAINING

The second stage of training concentrates on riding the horse through the bit. Once the horse is freely forward in the stretched or lower position, Phase II can begin.

When the horse lengthens down in Phase I, it stretches the long carrying muscles—the longissimus dorsi—along each side of the spine. The longissimus dorsi is the largest muscle in the horse's body, extending from the poll to the sacrum. Through small bundles of muscle fibers, the longissimus dorsi connects each vertebra to the next. By in large the strength of this muscle determines the elevation of the forequarters. These "bundles" of muscles can act independently of each other, either holding the spine rigid or allowing the spine to flex and articulate with the ribs.

In conjunction with the longissimus dorsi, the obliguus abdominis externus muscles form the abdominal wall. These muscles arc the back into longitudinal bend. As the horse rides through the bit and into a working frame, these muscles strengthen along with the other back and haunch muscles. This enables the horse to round his back and, by doing so, shift his balance further back from the forehand. As this occurs, the gait collects and the head and neck rise.

The same exercises that relax and flex also build strength once the horse's spine is correctly aligned and he begins to utilize his back and haunch. Strengthening begins when the horse comes through the bit.

Fanny demonstrates the trot in Phase II. She is starting to engage her hind end and use her back, allowing her energy to flow, which gives the gait its nice appearance.

Experience has shown me that many riders fall into the rut of using too much leg and too much rein, sending the horse into a downward spiral of resistance and evasion. It takes a unique rider to master the sport through strength. That is why, in my opinion, comparatively few are highly successful. I believe horses are more capable and more willing to perform out of gymnastic preparation than from the driving force of the rider.

Here, Fanny has fallen forward and flattened through her back. During Phase II training, the rider continually helps the horse to rebalance more to the haunch. It is through this process that the horse learns to carry himself.

Initially, maintaining the Phase II position will be intermittent, but it will build into a working frame as the horse carries each incremental change in balance.

Many riders are taught to drive and hold in order to put the horse into a working frame. Indeed, one can achieve a working frame by using different methods than those described in this book. Lightness, however, asks the rider to look at the concepts of "forward" and what is commonly called "on the bit" in specific ways. Lightness applies to all the aids—the hand, seat or body, and leg. The rider's leg and seat remain relaxed—not attempting to drive—but encourage the horse to bring himself forward. When the horse drives himself, he also balances himself.

The intention of lightness is that there be no resistance in the rein. In the term *on the bit,* the word *on* by definition implies support; that is, the horse uses the bit for support to some degree. The preposition *through* in the terms *through the bit* or *through the hand* carries the meaning *without stopping* and indicates that the bit does not stop the horse's energy. While *on the bit* and *through the bit* are each used as confirmation that the horse accepts the bit, the variation in terminology identifies philosophical differences in training methods.

Summary of Phase II:
- A combination of aids (see Working In Hand) asks the relaxed horse to flex at the poll and release into the forward movement. The rider feels intermittent balance and support under her seat as the horse reaches forward into a relaxed jaw.
- Lateral gymnastic exercises supple and strengthen, giving the rider access to the placement of the horse's shoulders and hind legs.
- With the horse in better alignment, the rider can collect the horse's stride, increasing his degree of self-carriage.
- The horse can remain on the aids for longer lengths of time. With increased suppleness and strength, he can begin to make transitions without sacrificing relaxation or balance.
- The rider works less when the horse remains on the aids. Once the horse remains balanced, the aids becomes increasingly lighter.

PHASE III TRAINING

The final segment of the training begins once the horse is relaxed and on the aids most of the time. By Phase III the horse is schooling all the lateral exercises and has developed enough strength and suppleness to collect himself and balance in lightness much of the time (though not as competently or as fluidly as is ultimately desired).

During Phase III the rider builds upon the basic execution of the movements to solidify the horse to the aids. This happens through practicing transitions and introducing such advanced exercises as the collected canter, counter-canter, flying changes, and rein-back. The horse's strength and suppleness will increase through the deep engagement required by these exercises. This strength allows the horse to remain light and fluid for longer distances and provides the power to collect the gaits. With increased collection comes lift and the ability to attain the dramatic reach of stride that adds elegance to advanced work. When this enhanced gait is achieved through relaxation, the horse stays happily within his natural realm of movement and, consequently, light to the aids.

Summary of Phase III:

- This marks the time for dynamic strength-building and refinement of the aids. Horse and rider present a polished package.
- Advanced exercises increase the efficiency of energy flowing forward from the haunch.
- The rider's relaxation allows the horse's energy to flow through her seat, creating communication so sensitive that there is constant lightness to all the aids.

Yoda demonstrates the strength and agility of Phase III.

CHAPTER 5

Working In Hand

*Like people, horses will sometimes make things far more compli-
cated than they need to be. Keep each process simple to allow
learning to have a controlled step-by-step progression.*

Much of the horse's reality is what the trainer creates. Everything
the trainer does at the beginning of training and throughout the
program matters, including the sequence of learning and how each
exercise is introduced. Patience and preparation are essential in order
to give the horse the best advantage for success.

All horses, whether green or mature, benefit from time spent in
hand. In most cases it is easier for the horse to begin relaxation,
stretching, and flexion without the weight of the mounted rider.
Suppling and flexing the horse's body in hand provides the foundation for learning under saddle. In this respect it is worth noting that
how a horse responds in hand is normally a good indication of what
he will accomplish under saddle. The rider also benefits: By handling
the horse in hand, she can identify baseline flexibility and strength.

BEGINNING IN HAND

In-hand exercises have both training and gymnastic value: Relaxing a
muscle increases its ability to stretch; stretching or "opening" the muscle allows it to return to its natural length with increased blood flow to
the tissues; and flexion allows the horse to work in the correct position to build strength.

To encourage the horse to utilize his back, begin each exercise
with the horse's jaw relaxed and the head and neck in the lowered

position, at or near level with the withers. To be effective in hand, the trainer needs the aid of a long dressage-style whip. The horse must learn to move forward from a touch on top of the croup, laterally from a touch on the side, and stop or back up from a touch on the chest. The whip becomes an invaluable aid once the horse understands it as nothing more than an extension of the trainer's reach.

Before training can begin, the horse must regard the whip as an aid. Some horses have an innate fear of the whip or a fear that stems from prior misuse of the whip. This needs to be overcome because the horse won't relax or learn when he's afraid. To gain respect, use the whip with light touches, just as you would touch with your hand or leg. At any time, if a touch doesn't produce a response, awaken the horse to the lesson with two or three rapid taps in succession. After such an "awakening," always rub the whip gently across the body until relaxation is regained. Rubbing the whip on the croup is particularly comforting to the horse.

Some horses will need their entire bodies desensitized to the whip. This can take many sessions of methodically touching and rubbing the whip over each part of the body. Using the whip in this fashion instills respect for both the whip and the trainer without causing fear.

The trainer's position changes with respect to the horse as each in-hand exercise is taught and progresses. If the horse has no knowledge of what is expected, stand close to his body to help flex and guide him in the right direction. In this closer position, the whip isn't helpful. Instead, the trainer uses the weight or pressure of her hand to influence the horse. Once the general direction of the exercise is determined, stand back to establish a better training position. As necessary, the whip may be used to extend reach. Riders not accustomed to handling the long whip should practice moving the aid smoothly around the horse.

Each exercise is taught in the same manner, whether in hand or under saddle. Inaugurally, the horse is taught to respond correctly to the aid. Then the trainer deliberately slows the delivery of the exercise in order to ensure that each step of the movement is correct. Once the movement is correct, the horse can be more forward in his delivery. The trainer starts each new exercise by asking the horse for only one or two good steps at a time, but gymnastic benefit increases exponentially once the horse can maintain a series of good steps together.

To continue any exercise when the horse is technically incorrect does more harm than good. Because the horse learns through repetition, every time the trainer/rider allows the horse to practice the wrong way, it becomes, in effect, what is taught—and it becomes a habit. Furthermore, it can be difficult to correct a bad position midstream. Using discipline only creates confusion. Remember, the horse is rarely wrong: Either his interpretation of what the trainer expects is incorrect, or he is physically unable to do what is asked. The trainer needs to put the horse into the correct position to perform properly, then only ask for a level of delivery he can maintain.

Asking that progress be achieved on the horse's terms need not incur delays or stagnation. The trainer ought to regularly test the horse's capabilities to improve and advance. This requires the trainer to "listen" to the horse's body. Keep in mind that the horse must remain within the natural realm of his true movement; it is here that he relaxes and advances.

Expect the horse to be more supple in one direction than the other. Avoid overworking the "good" side, believing that this will develop a better understanding of the movement and therefore improve the delivery on the weaker side. Instead, this creates an even bigger discrepancy from one rein, or bend, to the other. Work the weaker rein to be on a par with the stronger side. This may mean working longer in one direction before the horse relaxes or moves in a good frame with fluid rhythm. Measure success from the difficult side, being mindful that the horse is working harder in that direction.

The suppling process begins with relaxing the jaw. Relaxation leads to flexibility, which leads to balance, which in turn produces strength. Relaxation takes place throughout all three training phases. As the horse becomes confident in each phase, his degree of relaxation increases. The in-hand exercises progressively affect, or give access to, the horse's body in the following ways:

- Relaxing the jaw promotes bitting compliance; releasing at the occipital poll allows access to the vertebra of the neck.

- Lengthening the horse down accesses the spine and begins to stretch the top line. It also encourages the horse to step his hind legs deeply beneath his barrel.
- Shoulders-in rotations of the haunch around the shoulders supples the neck, opens the chest, and articulates the pelvis. The horse steps deeply underneath himself with the inside hind leg, then stretches out into the rotation. The lateral bend centers the deeper engagement under the spine.
- Counter-shoulders-in adjusts the shoulders through rotations around the haunch. This supples and prepares the horse to carry more weight behind the withers.
- Longe training articulates the rib cage from side to side and places the hind legs in spinal alignment for both lateral and longitudinal bend. Attaching side reins after the horse has stretched down in a long-and-low frame can help relax his body into a working frame.

Each trainer/rider will start the program with different expectations. By placing emphasis on the basics, this system aspires to the highest level of achievement, or the grand prix. While not every horse or rider will reach this summit of performance, the horse will have the tools to succeed and will not be held back from becoming even more accomplished at any time in the future. Solid training lasts a lifetime. Even when left unridden for a period of time, the horse will retain that knowledge and come back into form quickly.

THE TMJ (TEMPOROMANDIBULAR JOINT)

Because lightness begins at the jaw, it is important to have a basic understanding of how the TMJ and the teeth interact—or interfere— with jaw movement and ultimately the horse's willingness to flex and come forward through his back and through the bit.

The jaw needs a certain amount of lateral freedom in order to move from side to side. The horse's lower jaw must also "slip" from front to back. Freedom in these movements will incline the horse to lift and savor the bit with his tongue.

The hooks and ramps that develop on horses' teeth over time can impede movement in the jaw and also cause the horse discomfort. These growths lock up the temporomandibular joint, known as the TMJ.

The TMJ is one of three closely related joints. The atlanto-occipital joint, which allows the head front-to-back movement, is located between the occiput and atlas vertebra. The atlanto-axial joint, which controls the side-to-side movement of the head, is located between the first cervical vertebra, or atlas, and the second cervical vertebra, or axis. Since all three joints participate in aligning the vertebral column, any constriction in the TMJ has far-reaching consequences for how the horse works under saddle. Proper jaw movement is critical to the bitting process.

How the horse responds to the bit is intricately linked to relaxing and aligning the spine. If the movement of the jaw is restricted by blocks—ramps and hooks—or worse, a lock in the TMJ, it precludes a fluid release to rein pressure. Without ease of jaw movement, the horse will bump the rein, that is, he is not able to release the jaw to absorb pressure in the rein. When this happens over and over during every ride, the horse cannot relax or work with the rider in any meaningful way. If the rider fails to recognize the real problem, the horse's reaction might be misinterpreted as fighting or evading the aids, resulting in frustration for both horse and rider. Little positive training can be accomplished under these circumstances. Keep in mind that this type of restricted movement may be subtle and go unnoticed by an inexperienced rider. Although the horse might go on to perform satisfactorily, he may not reach his full potential.

In addition to the problem of hooks and ramps, chomping or violently chewing the bit is constricting to the jaw and indicates tension. Savoring the bit or "smiling" is a sign of relaxation or yielding and is the desired response. As the lessons in lightness proceed, most horses that are disposed to chomp the bit will lose their tenseness or apprehension and hold the bit quietly.

Maintaining the horse's teeth is about much more than good digestion. Horses of any age will need help to relax comfortably into the bit.

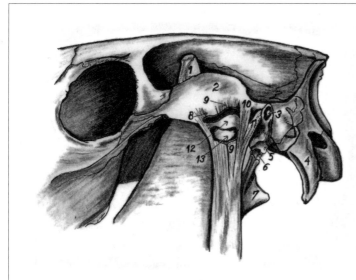

Temporomandibular articulation, left view:
1. Coronoid process of mandible
2. Zygomatic process of temporal bone
3. External acoustic opening
4. Paracondyloid process
5. Styloid process
6. Tympanohyoid
7. Stylohyoid
8. Lateral ligament
9. Articular capsule
10/11. Caudal ligament
12. Articular disc
13. Mandibular condylar

The view is opened to expose the articular disc and mandibular condylar. It is important to have pressure distributed equally between the horse's teeth and the TMJ. Whole-mouth dentistry can promote relaxation and flexion by eliminating discomfort with the bit and allowing full articulation of the TMJ.

Free articulation improves the TMJ function as a nerve center. Proprioception gives the horse a blind awareness of his leg movement and hoof placement. This "sixth sense" comes from nerves in the poll and hyoid apparatus of the TMJ. The coordination between these nerve centers can improve the horse's stride and balance. When the bridle pulls the bit too tightly, the consequences are twofold: The headstall can exert too much pressure on the nerves at the poll and/or restrict the tongue to lift and savor the bit to relax the jaw.

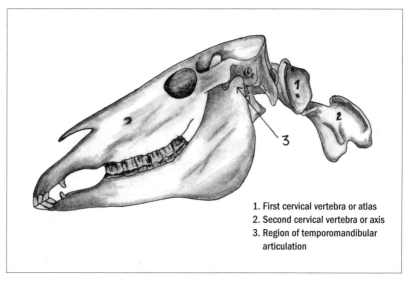

1. First cervical vertebra or atlas
2. Second cervical vertebra or axis
3. Region of temporomandibular articulation

Skull, left view with atlas and axis attached. Viewing the skull with the spinal connection demonstrates the relationship between the TMJ, the atlas, and the axis.

Seek out an equine dental practitioner who understands the concept of savoring the bit to achieve proper release to the TMJ. Then retain good functionality through annual inspections.

The following pages explain how to execute each in-hand exercise. Keep in mind that in practice ground exercises will overlap with both training on the longe and riding in the Phase I position.

RELAXING THE JAW

All horses have some amount of inner tension that interferes with true relaxation. Even if the horse currently comes into a working frame, it doesn't necessarily mean the jaw or poll has relaxed. It depends on how the position was achieved. For example, the rider can pressure the horse onto the bit by driving forward with her leg and/or seat and by restraining with her hands, but, by nature, whenever force is used, a certain amount of tension will result. The horse can obey the rider and present a favorable frame without releasing any inner tension. Driving the horse forward is always a balancing act between the tension within the horse and the tension within the rider and requires the rider's finesse to achieve any degree of lightness. In any case the horse is not likely to be relaxed in the sense or extent described in this program.

Teaching the Exercise

Relaxing the jaw may seem quite simple, but it can be difficult for many trainers to accomplish. The exercise begins by asking the horse to "give" to the inside rein. Lift the inside rein so that it slides upward on the ring of the bit. Vibrate the rein into the upper corner of the mouth until the horse mouths the bit. This indicates a release. When the horse makes this gesture, stop all movement of the rein.

Be careful not to push or pull the horse into a response by using force on the rein. If the horse learns or already expects to be pulled, the trainer will always be pulling, and the horse will never be light. On the other hand, once alert for a most subtle of aids, a slight vibration of the rein will gain the horse's attention and produce a response. Accept any modest offer of release and build upon that response. Repeat the process (in combination with the next exercise of lengthening the horse down) until it becomes second nature for the horse to give or flex the jaw every time the reins are lifted and/or vibrated. If the horse doesn't respond to the initial vibrations, keep repeating. Some horses won't immediately understand that such subtlety requires action. The trainer will need patience to start

First attempts to release the jaw will meet with resistance. Lift and vibrate the rein up into the inside corner of the mouth until the horse releases.

As the horse relaxes his jaw, release the rein to confirm that he has made the correct response.

the process. This small step begins the process that leads to greater and greater gain.

Ask the horse to relax to the vibration of each inside rein one rein at a time. The trainer should stand near the inside rein, leaving the opposite rein loose. This position encourages the horse's nose to move

Holding the reins longer brings the neck into the release. Releasing to the inside rein prepares the horse to lengthen down to stretch the neck and spine.

Vibrating both reins under the throatlatch will release the TMJ. By mouthing the bit, the horse confirms an understanding of how to release the TMJ in relaxation.

inward toward the trainer. Even though the trainer does not direct the nose toward her, the horse will tend to flex that way. Don't ask the horse to bring his head to a vertical position or try to hold the released position. The goal of this exercise is very simple—the horse gives to the vibration of the rein by demonstrating a release or mouthing the bit. If this causes the horse to bring the nose in, which it may, allow his head back to a natural angle when the aid is stopped. Don't make the exercise more complicated than it is.

Initially the trainer should hold the rein fairly close to the bit. Once the horse consistently offers a response from that position, hold the rein further away from the bit until they can be held near the withers. This will allow the trainer to put the horse in motion.

Asking the horse to release the jaw while both horse and trainer walk in the manège is the next step. When walking, the horse should be actively forward. Vibrating the rein is not an indication to move slowly or to stop. It is a request for relaxation only. If necessary, touch the horse's haunch with a long whip to maintain a forward direction. Hesitation to walk forward may indicate that the trainer is pulling back on the rein. The vibration of the rein should be in an upward direction and be so subtle that it may take time to summon a response.

Ask for the release to the rein as the horse walks forward.

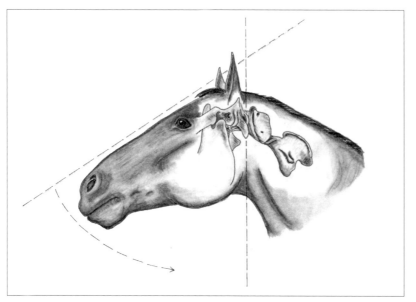

Head movement: The first cervical vertebra brings the horse to a near-vertical head carriage. When obtained through relaxation at the poll, the nose will simply relax down.

I talked about the jaw having an impact on spinal alignment when I discussed the TMJ. The first cervical vertebra controls the horse's back-to-front head movement. Once you relax the jaw, that nodding response tells you the horse will release at the poll (and therefore at C1, the first vertebra) when he feels pressure. That is all you want to accomplish right now.

The trainer must resist the temptation to pull the horse into a reaction to the rein, because it will disturb any measure of relaxation.

In order for the horse to release and savor the bit properly, he must trust·that the vibrations of the rein will not be followed by pulling of the rein. If he clenches his jaw, the trainer may hear him grinding his teeth or see a tightening of the muscles on the side of the jaw. This indicates a resistance to savoring the bit, which could be a habitual reaction to the rein. Repeat the exercise for as long as is necessary to build his confidence.

This humble start prepares the horse to stay relaxed throughout all the trainer/rider asks him to do. Take this simple exercise seriously and be patient with the horse; it may take time for him to understand. Use short teaching sessions over several days.

LENGTHENING DOWN

Lengthening or stretching the head and neck down is how the longitudinal gymnastic process begins. Lowering the head and neck stretches the entire top line. As the horse stretches in this manner, the relaxation created in the jaw begins to extend through the body.

When the horse relaxes and gives his jaw, releasing the rein encourages the head to drop. Allowing the rein to follow any downward movement sends the head even lower to the ground. The level of relaxation determines the degree of response.

Remember that the exercises are designed to supple the horse from front to back, stretching to relax each targeted part of the body. By lengthening the neck down, the horse stretches the muscles along the length of the spinal column. Walking the horse in this lengthened position encourages the stretched muscles to release tension.

Teaching the Exercise

Begin walking the horse in the manège. Slide the inside rein up on the ring of the bit, vibrating the corner of the mouth to relax the jaw. The

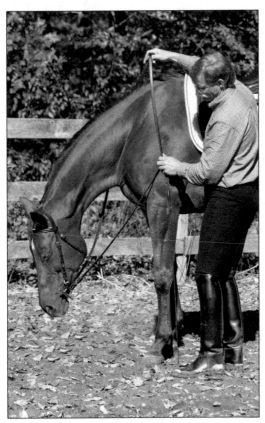

Once the horse will release in the jaw, lifting the outside rein connects him to the bit. Then, by releasing the reins, the horse will follow the rein down.

release to the inside rein will result in slight flexion, lightly connecting the outside rein. As the horse feels the outside rein, allow him to take the rein down by releasing both reins.

By vibrating only the inside rein aid, the trainer induces a small degree of bend in the horse's neck, prompting a downward motion. If the horse is relaxed to the bit, his head will sink. The trainer follows the horse's motion down by letting the reins slide through her fingers until the head stops sinking. Both horse and trainer continue walking with the head in the lower position.

If the horse is unwilling to release down, the trainer can, at halt, use some downward weight on the rein or encourage the horse to lower his head by bending down with her body. Once he sinks his head and neck down, the trainer should start walking forward. Every time the horse raises his head, repeat the process of vibrating the inside rein up into the corner of his mouth, followed by releasing both reins to encourage him to lower his head. The goal of this exercise is to teach the horse to relax his neck and follow the rein down any time the trainer offers the rein. The horse needs to be willing to release down and carry this lower position whenever the trainer requests.

Keep in mind that the release of the rein is not a reward for relaxing the jaw. The purpose of releasing the rein is to stretch the neck down. This in-hand stretching exercise is the trainer's initial access to the horse's spinal column. It is vital to teach this lesson without the rider's weight on the horse's back.

Horses generally learn to release in the jaw and lengthen down quickly when the exercises are taught in conjunction with one another. Lightness is learned by repetition, however. Even once the horse knows how to respond correctly, don't expect the same level of lightness each time. Consistent lightness develops as training progresses.

The seeming simplicity of these first two exercises may not properly convey their significance. In fact, the concept of relaxing and

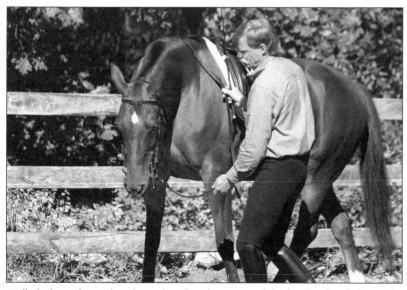

Walk the horse forward on the circle, asking him to stretch his head and neck down. The slight length bend of the circle facilitates softness and helps spread relaxation down the neck and spine. Here, Fanny shows an understanding of a full-body release as evidenced by the forward position of the inside hind leg. The horse is relaxed, soft, and through the back by virtue of releasing into the inside rein, then taking the outside rein down.

releasing to the rein sets a precedent that guides the horse throughout the entire training process and is the basis for him to achieve lightness. The trainer/rider should perform these two exercises whenever the horse is handled or ridden. Confirmation of both the release to the rein and willingness to lengthen down is vital to the success of all further training.

THE HALT

In an educated halt, the hind legs come forward and stop in balance under the horse. Pulling back on the rein actually interferes with the horse's effort to balance himself and is apt to create tension. Instead, closing the hand and fixing the rein on the withers allows the horse to step underneath his barrel; as he steps into the rein, he stops forward movement and halts. Fixing the rein, once the horse understands how to release to it, helps the horse maintain his balance.

Using incremental steps to change the way the horse thinks about balance and using his body works best. The smaller the change, the easier it is to affect his perception of balance and develop an academic approach to each movement.

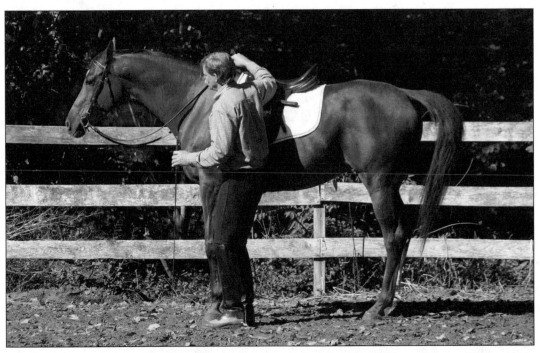

Halt in hand: Fanny has learned the halt and demonstrates stopping from the trainer's body suggestion—without weight in the rein. Note that the haunch is engaged without signs of resistance in the body.

Teaching the Exercise

Even in hand, the halt is considered a separate movement to be taught with the same attention to fundamentals as any other movement. Having already taught the horse to release to the rein, parameters are then established that tell the horse that he can't go past the fixed point of the rein.

Ideally, the trainer can walk the horse forward then close her fingers on the reins as each front leg comes forward. This on and off tension on the rein slows the front legs while allowing the hind legs to come underneath. If the horse doesn't stop, the trainer holds the rein in a fixed position by keeping her hand still, so the horse walks into the rein and halts. Later, when the trainer asks for a halt, the horse can respond without ever needing to feel more than a slight rigidity in the rein.

If the horse initially walks through the fixed position of the rein, the trainer can use a wall or fence to support the rein aid. As the horse walks toward the wall, begin closing the fingers on the rein on and off, then fix the rein two strides away from the wall. If the horse doesn't stop as he comes into the fixed rein, he must stop at the wall. Use this method until the horse relates to the aid and stops before reaching the wall. Take caution to apply the fixed rein properly. Fixing creates a "wall" to stop forward movement—the trainer does not pull back. If the horse tries to turn at the wall, insist that he remain straight. (Consider longeing to dissipate extra energy. Until he can relax and focus on the trainer, he lacks the mind-set to learn.)

Working in hand provides an opportunity to learn how to use your body as an effective aid. For example, stepping or leaning toward the horse's shoulder visually signals the horse to stop coming forward. If needed, touching the whip to the horse's chest (at the base of the neck) creates a "wall," teaching him about boundaries of space. Stepping or leaning toward the horse's hip will help move him back. Consistency with all the aids allows the horse to "read" the trainer and builds confidence in his own decision-making skills.

When the horse begins training, he may, at times, build up adverse or unusable energy. This nervous energy can be difficult to channel productively. By definition, nervous energy lacks relaxation, and the horse must relax to regain composure. When the horse can't dissipate extra energy into good movement, it can be best to put him on the longe. As the horse becomes academic, both horse and trainer/rider learn how to utilize all energy into the lesson while maintaining relaxation.

REIN-BACK

Rein-back has tremendous gymnastic benefits and is invaluable in every phase of training. At this early stage, it serves to teach the horse how to round his back and release through his pelvis. Correct delivery is complicated, however, and is all too often trained and performed incorrectly. Begin rein-back in hand once the horse correctly comes into the halt in hand.

Think of the movement as coming forward in reverse: The hindquarters lead the front end back. Conceptually, when impulsion comes from the haunch, there should be no difference in directing the motion either forward or backward. In contrast, the front end should never push against the haunch. This forces the horse back from the shoulder, making the haunch follow the movement rather than lead.

The trainer can make minute adjustments to the horse's position while working in hand. Halt and rein-back in hand provide an ideal platform for achieving delicacy in the aids and increasing the subtlety of movement—the horse learns to play with the possibilities of his own balance.

To help the horse understand this concept, the trainer must be able to distinguish stepping back from the haunch from pushing back from the shoulder. For example: If the trainer pulls back on the rein to initiate rein-back, the horse will move backward to release the pressure of the aid. Pulling the rein effectively asks the horse to push back from the shoulders, which is not what we want the horse to learn. Pulling a horse backward makes no more sense than pulling him forward. It is the indication of the aid, not force, that asks the horse to step backward. By closing the door to forward movement, backward movement becomes the next option. (For the advanced horse, elevation is also an option.)

Teaching the Exercise

Walk forward to halt with the horse in a long, low position and the jaw relaxed. Raise both reins so they slide up on the rings of the bit while saying "Back." Lightly use the whip to touch the chest; this contact should initiate a step back. The trainer moves with the horse, letting him halt and relax. If necessary, repeat the rein, voice, and whip aids until the horse steps back. The horse may offer more than one step, but do not ask for more steps during the first lesson. The trainer can further help the horse by leaning in the direction of the rein-back and stepping with the horse as he moves. This method uses several light aids and no pulling.

Initially, the horse may only respond to the touch of the whip. It may require a series of sessions for him to identify that the voice aid, as well as the lifting of the rein, represent the request to move. In time he will step back from the rein aid alone. He will also learn the trainer's voice command and respond to her body language. As the horse's response develops, slowly wean him from the whip aid until no whip is needed.

It is important to teach rein-back with the horse in the long-and-low position. This frame stretches the top line, encourages the back to

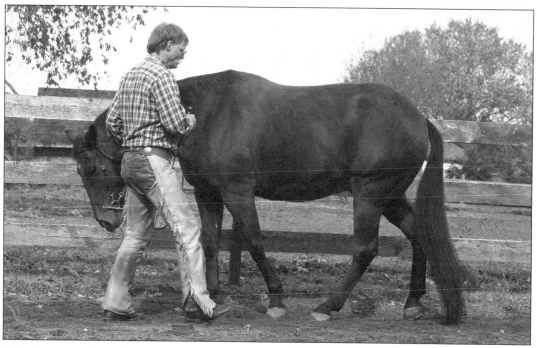

Yoda demonstrates how to begin rein-back in hand. Stretching down before asking for reverse prompts the horse to create motion from his haunch and not be tempted to push back from his shoulder.

rise and the pelvis to flex, and activates the hind legs. This disposition of the back, hip, and haunch is described as "coil" and is essential for gymnasticizing the hip and pelvis. Working in hand and without the saddle is the easiest way to teach the horse to utilize this position correctly. Even at an entry level, it is important that the horse uses his back in this manner.

From the time the horse can depart in a frame and step freely back without losing balance, coil and better utility of the back is developed. In addition, the horse learns to balance each step without looking to the rein for support.

For a moment let's return to the horse who was pulled backward by the rein. Pulling causes mental tension and muscle tightness throughout the neck and chest. In this state the horse is most likely to hollow his back behind the withers. (Other problems associated with tension of this sort are discussed in Body Mechanics of Horse and Rider.) In this hollowed-back position, it is easier for the horse to push back from the shoulders than to step backward from the haunch. Delivering rein-back in this manner is not only technically incorrect or false but would, over

When you feel the horse press into the rein, it means he has lost balance and is asking you to help him from falling farther forward onto his shoulder. Each time he releases to the rein, he learns more about relaxation and balance. This is an incremental process. The trainer/rider strives to help the horse into a better and better position until he is in an ideal self-carriage. You accomplish this by releasing the rein after the horse releases back first (thereby putting slack in the rein). You can maintain a fixed contact until he releases—just don't retract the rein to pull against him. Pulling when he leans into the rein teaches the horse to resist the pressure.

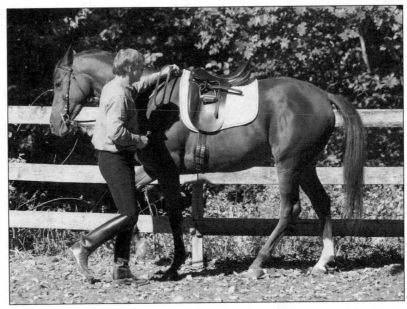

Fanny shows a clear understanding of the movement through her response to the trainer's body position. She is using her back without any weight in the rein to bring her back.

time, also develop the wrong muscle groups, making it even harder to correct at a later stage in the training program. Rein-back is an important lesson in balance; teaching it without a rounded back and stepping from the haunch negates any gymnastic value of the exercise.

Tilting the pelvis and rounding the back are what make rein-back such a powerful gymnastic tool. In this position the horse is poised not only to step backward from the haunch but also to utilize longitudinal bend in the forward gaits. Teaching rein-back in hand encourages the horse to develop this correct position. Later, when working the exercise under saddle, the horse will be better equipped to assume the same position. By that time the horse will have gained the strength to carry the rider in the raised, or engaged, position.

Rein-back is a two-beat gait in which the diagonal hoofs hit the ground at the same moment. To maintain coil and balance, it is crucial that this rhythm be correct. Initially, the trainer may need to encourage the two-beat rhythm with the whip. Once the horse sustains the rhythm, however, the backward steps should be slowed. Many horses will need to supple laterally (through shoulders-in) before reaching the degree of longitudinal bend required to sustain rein-back at a faster pace.

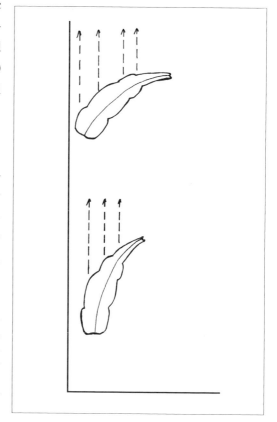

SHOULDERS-IN

Many trainers/riders identify shoulder(s)-in— and most lateral work, for that matter—only with performance dressage and do not recognize the gymnastic value of lateral work for horses of other disciplines. When the shoulders

Three-track versus four-track shoulders-in. Bend and angle are factors of lateral movement. Body suppleness allows bend to develop. Angulation (to the wall) develops lift by releasing the horse through the lower back. While the bend remains similar in either form of shoulders-in, the angle of the horse to the wall increases in the four-track version. Developing lift sooner helps to flex the horse's spine and increase his suppleness.

or the haunch are brought off the track (whether the horse moves into or away from the bend), the spine bends, the ribs articulate, and the body supples as a result. This so-called length bend is acquired through circles and lateral exercises. Length bend facilitates flexion and contributes to suppling the horse from front to back.

Lateral exercise can begin in hand after the horse relaxes the jaw and consistently follows the rein down to lengthen and stretch longitudinally. (This will most likely coincide with longeing and riding in the Phase I frame and starting rein-back in hand.)

Shoulder-in can be a three- or four-track movement, in which the horse's inside shoulder comes off a straight track. This system uses the plural, shoulders-in, to represent its preference for the four-track position in which both shoulders come off a straight track as much as forty-five degrees. Regardless of degree, the horse achieves length bend and moves in the opposite direction from his bend.

In classical training, shoulder-in is the most important suppling exercise. When the horse moves on four tracks, however, the increased angle serves to engage the inside hind leg further underneath the horse's body. This deeper engagement sets in motion the development of collection.

Bear in mind that the horse must be able to bend laterally in order to build the strength to effectively raise his back, or achieve longitudinal bend. Lengthening the horse down stretches and relaxes the horse's spine, a prerequisite to longitudinal bend. Rein-back also contributes to the development of longitudinal bend. But it isn't until shoulder(s)-in initiates lateral bend that longitudinal bend becomes meaningful in a gymnastic way. It is the combination of relaxed stretching of the spine with the engagement of the haunch that gives the trainer access to horse's back—and thus the key to longitudinal bend.

Training the horse in lightness introduces shoulders-in in hand from the *volte* by rotating the haunch around the shoulder. (Technically, a *volte* is a six-meter circle but in general terms can refer to a small circle of any size.) Using the *volte* makes teaching shoulders-in easy. Through rotation, the horse starts reaching and stretching both his shoulders and his haunch as well as articulating his rib cage.

Shoulders-in on the rotation does not look like what many riders think of as shoulder-in. The rotation allows both horse and trainer to explore the horse's range of motion, obtain deeper flexes, and maximize suppleness. These photos show the position of the horse with each stride. Beginning with the horse's head low helps him to utilize his back.

Teaching the Exercise

Start with the horse standing parallel to the wall about three feet from the track. The trainer stands on the inside near the withers. Use the inside rein to relax the jaw and create an inside bend in the poll and neck. Release the rein to lower the neck position near level with the withers. Next, the trainer steps back from the horse, bringing his shoulders one step with her. Then, touching with the long whip, she asks the horse to move his haunch to the outside (touch anywhere from the middle of the barrel up to the point of the hip, or wherever the horse responds).

Movement of the haunch creates a large turn around the shoulder. The shoulder must

mobilize and move with the haunch (moving both the shoulders and the hips away from the trainer as the horse turns), making a circle around the trainer. Each inside leg should cross over and in front of the outside leg. This leg action opens the chest as well as works the haunch. Do not allow the shoulder to drag behind the motion of the haunch (or vice versa).

The trainer uses the inside rein to create bend, taking the shoulders off the track, while at the same time supporting the bend with the outside rein. The gymnastic action of stepping the inside hock well under the barrel sinks the inside hip. Then, as that hoof pushes off the ground, it lifts the horse's back up and to the outside of the *volte*. As the exercise develops, more stretch and reach will place the inside hind leg farther under the horse, which, in turn, allows for more stretch and reach out of the movement with the outside leg. The reach of the horse's front legs should increase proportionately to that of the hind.

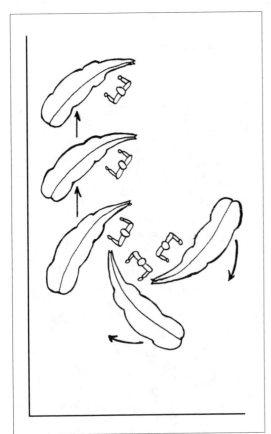

It is important for the jaw to stay relaxed during the rotation and to maintain bend at the poll. Do not twist the head or neck with the rein. Remember, the horse's neck should remain at or near level with the withers to work the movement through the back. (Teaching the horse to push his back up now makes him more likely to utilize his back correctly under saddle later.)

Remember that relaxation enhances suppleness and allows for increased flexion. The horse's response should be quiet but with deliberate energetic strides. Always be soft with the whip. Allow the horse to move himself—the whip is a directional aid, unless the horse drags his response. Never use the whip in a manner that prompts him to escape the aid.

Shoulders-in in hand: rotation to straight on the long wall.

Once movement becomes fluid on the rotation, change the delivery to the traditional straight line exercise. To do this begin a rotation into a corner of the manège. After the horse completes the corner and his shoulders come off the track, walk laterally down the manège in a straight line (against the wall). Begin with just a few strides. Return to the *volte* or walk off straight if correctness or freeness of movement is lost. The horse should maintain a rhythm of stride. Do not let the haunch drag behind the shoulder or escape to the outside. (Keeping the haunch close to the wall can help with engagement, but watch that length bend and the horse's body angle to the wall is maintained.)

Integrate shoulders-in, both on and off the circle, into the daily training routine. Work each rein and change direction frequently. In this system, shoulders-in can be done on a *volte* or a straight line. It is

I refer to the lateral exercises as the beginning of the strength-building process because lateral work, in total, should make up the largest percentage of the overall training time. The lateral movements under saddle are primary in the horse's gymnastic development.

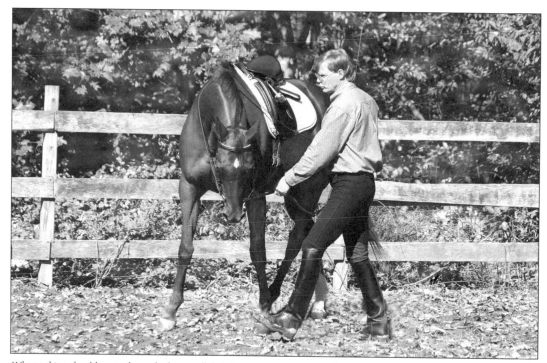

When taking shoulders-in down the long wall, it is important to maintain the release through the top line—and the release into the lateral bend. The stretch of the inside hind leg indicates the degree of relaxation through the hip. The lower position of the head, in combination with length bend, tends to relax the back and allows the inside leg to engage deeply. The horse's head will rise as the horse moves freely into the movement.

the gymnastic value of the movement, rather than the movement it-self, that is important.

Shoulders-in is a function of bend and angle: The bend is consistent in both the three- and four-track positions. The degree of suppleness determines the angle (the horse's position in relationship to the wall) in which the horse can move freely and, therefore, effectively engage. The degree of angle (up to forty-five degrees) represents the difficulty of the exercise—the greater the angle, the deeper the engagement. There is a direct relationship between angulation and flexion when asking the horse to engage.

The horse's willingness to step freely without changing frame (or later cadence) is key to maintaining his relaxation. This means shoulders-in might begin on three tracks. Increase the angle as the horse's comfort level changes and be sure to maintain the same angle on each rein in order to keep each side "on par" with the other.

COUNTER-SHOULDERS-IN

Counter-shoulders-in (also known as shoulder-out) is not natural for the horse in the wild. It requires the horse to initiate a turn from his outside shoulder, something he would not normally do. Nevertheless, this "unnatural" movement has far-reaching benefits in his gymnastic development and is fairly easy for the horse to learn.

Like shoulders-in, the horse moves away from the bend in counter-shoulders-in. When worked on a straight line, there is essentially no difference between the two exercises. On rotations, however, they are distinctly different: Shoulders-in rotates the haunch around the shoulder, gymnasticizing the haunch; counter-shoulders-in walks the shoulders around the haunch, developing the shoulder. Both exercises also unify the movement of the shoulder and the haunch, meaning that they develop the scope of sideways reach equally on both the front leg and the hind leg stride. Counter-shoulders-in teaches the horse to open the chest and loosen the elbow.

When working on the *volte*, the horse can't work in unity and still maintain a circle. Teaching both the exercises on the *volte*, however, where the shoulder and the haunch are emphasized separately, serves

Progression of shoulders-in depends largely on the innate or existing strength and flexibility of the horse. He must remain light and quiet in the bit, not raising his head or dropping the base of his neck or back. Stop the exercise if there is any deviation from the correct position. Walk the horse forward to regain his composure before starting again. Then, only ask for a movement he can maintain with a correct frame. Don't push him into repeating the same mistake. Make several rotations in each direction to establish the relationship between the aid and the response.

to equalize the horse's stride when asked to execute lateral exercises on a diagonal line such as half-pass.

An important goal of all lateral work is to allow the trainer to adjust the length and timing of the horse's stride (both back and front). The long-term benefits of this ability are far-reaching. If there is tightness within the horse's body, the timing of his stride will be off, hampering smooth movement. The ability to release tightness is mandatory for high-level work. For example, if the haunch drags behind the shoulder, working shoulders-in will loosen the stifle or hock. Likewise, if the shoulder is behind the motion, counter-shoulders-in frees the shoulder and elbow and opens the chest, allowing the rider to adjust the horse's forward stride and create fluidity of movement. In Phase III the exact timing of each hind leg stride is essential for executing such movements as flying changes. Teaching shoulders-in and counter-shoulders-in initiates the ability to adjust the horse with precision later on in the training process.

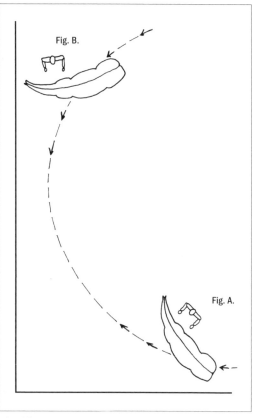

Shoulders-in versus counter-shoulders-in. Both shoulders-in and counter-shoulders-in move the horse away from the bend. Fig. A shows that shoulders-in walks the haunch to the outside of the shoulder. Fig. B shows that counter-shoulders-in places the shoulder to the outside of the haunch.

Teaching the Exercise

Teaching this movement in hand can be more difficult for the trainer than for the horse. First, it is important to allow plenty of room to rotate; plan to begin on a twenty-meter circle. Start from shoulders-in along the long side and work diagonally toward the center line. At the center line, take one step out in front of the horse's inside shoulder. In order to keep ahead of the horse's movement, the trainer must lengthen her stride as she steps the horse's shoulders around his haunch (maintaining the same bend as shoulders-in). The terms *inside* and *outside* refer to ther horse's bend rather than his position within the school.

The counter-shoulders-in rotation demonstrates how the horse moves the shoulder around the haunch. The circle needs to be large enough to maintain separation of all four legs so they may cross and step freely and independently.

As the previous diagram shows, the exercise requires the trainer to walk on a larger circle than the horse. Be careful not to increase the pace of your walk, as this will cause the horse to rush his delivery and subsequently lose relaxation and coordination. In order to cover extra ground, lengthen your stride while keeping all other variables of the movement constant.

The horse must maintain length bend in order to engage properly. Some horses may try to overbend the neck. This allows the horse to rotate with his body straighter, avoiding proper engagement. Watch the horse's entire position (not just his leg movement) to determine if he is performing correctly.

Keep in mind that counter-shoulders-in is not a turn on the haunch but a rotation of the shoulders around the haunch (just as the haunch rotated around the shoulders with shoulders-in). The exercise works the whole horse. Keep the jaw relaxed, the rein light in hand, and the neck at or near level with the withers.

To produce good clean steps, the horse may initially need help activating the haunch. Be ready to touch the inside hind leg or haunch with the whip to maintain impulsion. Keep the arc of the circle large enough so that the outside hock does not compress. The horse should

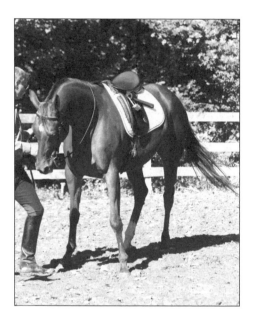

walk freely around. If the circle becomes too tight, the hock can twist to turn instead of stepping. The hoof should not swivel on the ground. Look for clean deliberate steps originating from the hip. (You may need to exaggerate the inside bend briefly to help the hind legs

Fanny shows what happens when the counter-shoulders-in rotation is too confining. Her legs remain together, causing the hock to compress as it turns and the shoulder to stick. Note the tenseness in the muscles of the barrel and haunch compared to the freedom of movement in the prior photo sequence.

step under the horse's body, but do not continue the exaggerated position any longer than is necessary to engage the haunch.)

Remember, this sequence of leg movement is foreign to the horse. He must be taught how to turn and cross his legs with an outside arc to his body. He may "stick" in the shoulder until he relaxes and remembers the movement. Sticking or hesitating indicates that the horse is having difficultly processing the exercise in his brain. The trainer can help by coming closer to the horse and prompting his shoulder with her hand. Patiently allow time for his thought process to coordinate with his leg movement.

The horse may stick in either the shoulder or the haunch when learning any of these different exercises. The hesitation may be a mental or physical block. By coming closer to the horse and helping him move, you reinforce relaxation and leadership without force.

HALF-PASS

Half-pass introduces forward movement into the bend. Like counter-shoulders-in, half-pass is not natural for horses in the wild, so the concept can be difficult for some horses to comprehend. The exercise combines the leg action learned in the last two exercises with new directional bend.

Looking in the direction of movement, half-pass requires the horse to step out into the bend with the inside shoulder (front leg), followed by the outside hind leg, which comes diagonally across. Then the opposite diagonal legs follow across together. The outside hind leg does two things: First it steps across into the bend in a sinking motion over and in front of the inside hind leg. Then it lifts as the inside hind leg steps out into the motion.

After the trainer establishes the correct position to work counter-shoulders-in in hand, managing half-pass in hand is easier. An effective way to teach half-pass in hand starts from the counter-shoulders-in position.

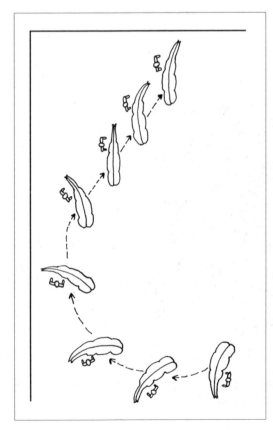

Use counter-shoulders-in to half-pass when the horse is fluid on a small rotation.

Teaching the Exercise

Begin counter-shoulders-in on a ten-meter circle along the short side of the manège once the horse passes the center line. As the horse circles, his body will become parallel to the long wall. From here, move the horse diagonally toward the center line. Now, take two or three strides to change the horse's bend. The act of changing bend while maintaining forward movement sends the horse diagonally toward the center line in half-pass.

Initiate the change of bend through the rein aids—remember that the terms *inside* and *outside* follow the bend. What is the outside rein in counter-shoulders-in becomes the inside rein in half-pass. The trainer changes the bend to the new inside rein while allowing the horse to take the new outside rein. As the horse steps into the new bend, he steps into the half-pass position. End half-pass after two or three strides by walking straight forward.

The purpose of teaching half-pass in hand is only to introduce the horse to the concept of moving forward into the bend. Taking two or three good steps at a time is sufficient to accomplish the goal; it is unnecessary to train this exercise in long sessions. While half-pass in hand isn't developed to the same level as the other exercises, it is essential to acquaint the horse in hand before asking for the movement with the weight of the rider in the saddle.

If trainer or horse has trouble making the transition from counter-shoulders-in directly into half-pass as described above, a different progression may prove easier: Move in shoulders-in off the center line and walk diagonally

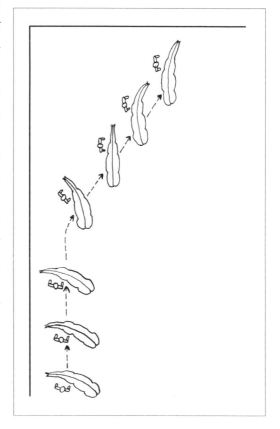

Shoulders-in to half-pass. Starting half-pass from this shoulders-in position along the center line will help the trainer who is having trouble going all the way around the corner in counter-shoulders-in.

toward the long wall. When horse and trainer are comfortable moving diagonally toward the wall—away from the bend—use the outside rein to straighten the bend. After the horse straightens, use the same rein to acquire the new bend into the direction of movement—this is now the inside rein. He is in half-pass at the point where the horse moves into his bend.

Keep an eye on the haunch throughout the movement. Some horses tend to focus on the shoulder and lose the haunch position. Others try to lead with the haunch. While the shoulder must lead, the impulsion still comes from behind. When working in hand, the trainer keeps the haunch active by supporting the horse's movement with the whip (possibly resting the whip at the horse's hip). Only tap with the whip if the movement slows, or when the haunch fails to keep up with the shoulder. Teaching half-pass through progressions of counter-shoulders-in and shoulders-in shows the horse how to move forward regardless of bend. Accomplishing a fluid change of bend is all that is necessary in hand.

Working half-pass in hand also benefits the trainer/rider. It helps dramatize the concept of giving the inside rein to send the horse into

When moving the horse in half-pass in hand, the trainer merely directs the horse to move into the bend.

the bend, which is the most advanced aid for initiating half-pass under saddle. Because the rider teaches bend with the inside rein and her inside leg, there is a tendency to continue using the same aids even once bend and lateral direction are established. It is important to remember, however, that as the inside rein flexes the horse, it is the "giving" inside rein that allows the movement to form. The horse must be taught the concept of seeking bend from the outside rein. Delivery of half-pass explains the point: When the rider creates the bend for half-pass by overusing the inside rein, she effectively pulls the horse forward with the rein. In hand, with the trainer positioned at the horse's outside shoulder, it is impossible to send the horse diagonally forward by pulling the inside rein. Releasing the inside rein teaches the horse to create bend from slack in the outside rein. The trainer's position in hand, walking at the horse's shoulder, helps send the horse into half-pass, thereby teaching the horse to bend by taking the outside rein. This lesson is invaluable for an advanced understanding of bend.

SUMMARY OF WORK IN HAND

Collectively, the in-hand exercises teach the horse to work in relaxation, to gain alignment through flexion, and to balance various movements of the shoulder and the haunch. All three components are equally important. Lateral work in hand also allows the trainer to begin to place the shoulder and the haunch in specific ways. Command of the in-hand exercises will smooth the transition into mounted work.

A book can only discuss one exercise at a time. In practice the trainer adds exercises to the daily routine as the horse progresses. Utilizing all the exercises within a working session adds measurably to the overall benefit. Changing the bend and varying the movements produces the maximum suppleness and awareness to the aids. While working the in-hand exercises, the horse can also be working on the longe and riding circles in the Phase I position. Typically, time spent on longe work decreases as the horse advances on the circle under saddle. The amount and frequency of time spent on lateral work in hand will depend on the individual horse. Some horses need to supple in hand before and/or at the end of each ride.

Because the horse learns and develops each lesson in a methodical manner, he will learn faster if the trainer adheres to a training sequence: First, teach the correct response to the aids; second, slow the delivery to gain correctness; and finally, add more duration once the horse can balance and move fluidly in the exercise.

Throughout the learning process, focus on the three stages of gymnastic development—relaxation, flexion, and strength-building. Allow sufficient time in each stage—the horse has to learn and gain muscle memory to carry out the exercises. Flexing and balancing is at times difficult, and, quite naturally, evasions will surface. While working in hand, pay particular attention not to overflex the neck or allow the horse's head or neck to twist. This may happen as the horse is learning, but it can also result if the trainer is aggressive with the aids. Watch that the horse's ears remain level as he flexes—this is an indication that the bend is correct. A smooth and equal length bend is evidence of his proficiency, suppleness, and general understanding.

Relaxation is measured by the horse's response to any aid—he should take action willingly. Where there is resistance, there is tension or misunderstanding. Look to develop steady deliberate steps even if it means the delivery is slow. The trainer needs to differentiate slow but deliberate action from that which lacks purpose. If the latter, the horse needs to be motivated to come forward without losing relaxation. "Forward" will evolve into impulsion once flexion and strength develop his balance. In hand and during Phase I, impulsion is less critical in this system. The horse need only be energized to understand forward.

The horse is forward if he is able to adjust his stride—shortening or lengthening slightly within a gait—without disturbing the rhythm of the gait. This also confirms relaxation. Advocating free and forward movement, however, does not mean the horse is allowed to quicken his stride. Rushing is usually a sign of confusion or that an aid has been applied too strongly. Hurriedness disrupts correctness, which results in poor performance. Encourage free and forward movement within the sphere of relaxation that the horse can maintain.

Some horses will end in-hand sessions highly stimulated. This doesn't necessarily mean a loss of relaxation—it can represent the horse's motivation to perform and is considered a good response. It's important, however, to decompress this energy before continuing other training or retiring for the day. Lengthen the horse down by releasing the jaw and allowing the reins to follow the head and neck down. This releases tension and clears the mind by stretching the spinal column. The horse should stretch down whenever the trainer/rider asks; if he does not respond, he is not sufficiently relaxed.

Ground work also affords the trainer an opportunity to learn relaxation herself. Her relaxation on the ground is equally as important as it is in the saddle. The old masters called this "mastery of self," and it is essential for the horse's success. "Mastery of self" refers to the trainer's overall composure—control of her reflexes, reactions, responses, and fears. Once the trainer is in control of herself, then she can lead.

Horses will test the trainer's leadership. If she fails to lead, then the issue over authority may become confrontational. While complying with most aids, some horses will try to dominate whenever they deem a lesson too difficult. In hand, this is frequently demonstrated by crowding into the trainer's space or pushing her away. Unquestionably, the horse has the ability to overpower the trainer, so address any issue of authority swiftly. (If you can't take control of the horse quickly, ask a professional trainer to help you learn to lead and to correct the horse's behavior. Don't risk getting hurt.) Control has little to do with force—it refers to the horse's willingness to subordinate to the trainer as the leader of their partnership. When the trainer controls her "self," she controls the horse. Control on the ground gains his respect and carries over into mounted work.

CHAPTER 6

Longeing

The horse's point of view is an important part of the equation. If he isn't working with you, you work against him.

Longe training is an integral part of educating the horse. It introduces the horse to the dynamics of the circle while maturing the relationship between horse and trainer. Longeing not only allows the horse to find elementary bend and balance before carrying the weight of a rider, but also over a period of time helps the trainer develop an eye for how the horse moves, responds, and learns. Horses of any age and background will benefit from work on the longe.

Observation is a powerful teacher: Watching the horse respond on the longe lets the trainer visualize what she will feel in the saddle. Seeing the horse drop his shoulder, for instance, and then learn to keep his body level, signals the trainer to make similar corrections later under saddle. Such observations will also enable the rider to predict a loss of balance or an evasion before it happens. Studying the horse's every muscle line and the way each foot falls sensitizes the trainer to the horse's body and allows her to monitor the changes that occur as relaxation, flexibility, and strength develop.

One of the first assessments to make is how left- or right-sided the horse is. Like humans, horses normally favor one side, and as with people, this one-sidedness can result in unequal muscle development. Disparities from one side to the other will make the horse stiff or crooked. When coupled with the rider's natural one-sidedness, variations in the horse's movement from one rein to the other can be quite dramatic. Fortunately, increasing relaxation and flexibility alleviates stiffness and helps to equalize movement on each rein.

Although a tremendous amount of training can eventually be accomplished on the longe, starting the teaching process can be challenging. Many of us have memories of gazing out the classroom window completely detached from the teacher on the other side of the room. A similar disconnect frequently occurs when the horse is at the other end of the longe line.

All horses are distracted at times, but some will have real difficulty paying attention. As the team leader, the trainer needs to provide an atmosphere conducive to learning. Select an appropriate training site where there are few distractions. The enclosed space of a round pen or an arena best directs the horse's attention inward on the trainer. Training on the longe requires structure and the same discipline as training under saddle. Give the horse time to understand the longeing process before exposing him to external stimuli. Once he trusts your guidance, he will be more likely to focus on the aids. "Seasoning" the

A safe and quiet spot helps the horse relax and focus on learning.

horse to maintain composure in distracting situations comes after he knows how to respond to the aids.

EQUIPMENT

Proper equipment is also essential for successful results.

Longe line. Use a heavy webbed line with a normal snap at the end. The wind can pick up a lightweight line, and when the line flutters or sails, unwanted or confusing signals are sent to the horse. A weighty line, such as one with a chain at the end of the line, is also a poor choice because the trainer's subtle vibrations of the line cannot reach the horse. Most importantly, lightness cannot be taught with a chain over the horse's nose or poll.

Longeing surcingle with multiple side-rein fittings. To improve the alignment of the spine, the horse's body must be channeled into a precise position for work on the longe. This means connecting side reins at an exact angle. A saddle can be a functional alternative, but you won't achieve the same degree of precision or be able to replicate fittings from one lesson to another.

Side reins. Use solid leather adjustable straps. The objective of the side rein is to teach the horse how to release the pressure of the rein. When the horse relaxes his jaw, tension in the rein ceases. Avoid stretchable reins or reins with elastic inserts of any kind because the stretch mechanism will hold some tension on the rein even as the horse releases. The horse benefits from a learning process that is black or white—either there is tension in the rein or there is no tension. An elastic connection adds an area of gray—having less tension. This ambiguity interferes with the horse's long-term decision-making process.

Longe whip. Any style of long longeing whip is acceptable.

Longeing caveson. Being able to attach the longe line to a front ring of the noseband is extremely helpful. This connection positions the horse to follow his nose. In lieu of a caveson, attach the longe line to the bottom chin ring of any ordinary halter placed over the bridle so that the side reins can still be attached to the rings of the snaffle.

Some riders consider side reins with elastic inserts a kinder and gentler method to position the horse in a working frame. If you have ever pushed against a horse, you know that his innate response is to push back. Similarly, the horse will lean on the rein for balance if allowed. Teaching lightness asks that the horse always release to pressure of any kind.

TEACHING TO LONGE

Teaching lightness is as true on the longe as it is under saddle: Voice, body, line, and whip aids are combined to provide guidance to the horse. The trainer's actions should always be soft but deliberate. The commands to walk, trot, canter, or halt need to be clearly and consistently enunciated in order for the horse to understand and act on them.

It is also important that the trainer stays centered in the circle and centered to the horse. Face the horse, just behind the shoulder, so you won't be either in front of or behind the motion. Relax your arms, and keep them at your side.

The horse must learn to circle on the line and understand longe commands before he is asked to modify his position through the connection of the side reins. However, tacking with the surcingle and unconnected side reins from the onset can be beneficial. The hooks and straps will jostle about, making noise with the horse's movement. Having this distraction when everything is new avoids disrupting the horse's relaxation later in the process.

The longe line itself is used to communicate both deliberate and subtle messages. The trainer must hold the line firmly enough so the horse can't pull the line outward to expand the circle, yet still be able to communicate through the line. Vibrating the line sends a "heads-up" signal to the horse that another command is coming. Remember, the horse learns even these delicate gestures by repetition, so consistency is important. Working with precision in hand and on the longe allows the horse to focus on the softness of each aid, which will extend to work under saddle.

The whip serves as an extension of the trainer's arm and as an aid to motivate the

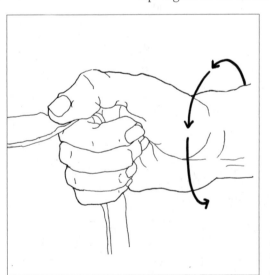

Rolling the longe line in a circular motion (in the direction of the horse's movement) subtly lengthens his top line and moves the gait forward. This is consistent with lengthening down in the Phase I frame. Illustration: Cecily L. Steele

horse forward. Although each trainer will doubtless develop an individual longeing style, pointing the whip at the haunch while saying "Walk" or "Trot" should be sufficient to prompt an upward gait change. Likewise, looping the end of the whip in a circular motion toward the horse while saying "Canter" should motivate that gait change without overly exciting the horse or being confrontational. When the whip is not being used, keep it pointed down.

The cardinal rule of longeing is to keep the circle round. The horse does not benefit from circle training if allowed to describe only roundish shapes. To make a circle round, the trainer must remain centered in the circle. For a correct circle to form, the longe line must stay equally taut as the horse moves all the way around. Don't put the horse on a track too large or too small for his ability.

Changing rein on the longe is simply redirecting the horse's forward movement. To begin, bring the horse to a halt on the circle. Walk to him and physically turn him (moving inward) to face the other direction. Then, walk back to the center of the circle before asking him to go forward. Once the horse can halt and stand on the circle, the trainer can remain at the center to change direction. Moving backwards encourages the horse to turn in and face the trainer. Once he faces in, pointing the whip toward the "new" inside shoulder will send him forward on the other rein. As he learns the aids, the change of rein will become fluid. Because horses learn to read body language well, longeing can elevate this talent to an art for both horse and rider.

CONNECTING THE SIDE REINS

Training lightness asks the horse to learn a new balance on his own terms, not by applying force or by restraint. The trainer/rider offers the horse choices, then assists him in making the right decisions. Side reins don't pull the horse into position, they offer him a choice: He can either maintain his current balance with some discomfort or eliminate the tension in the rein by making a slight change in position. To make changing position the horse's choice, ask only for small and easily attained changes. Whenever the horse is overwhelmed by change, leaning into pressure may seem to him the better option.

Until the horse understands length bend, the trainer must control the circle. Don't allow the horse to change the circle by pulling out or drifting in—he's just avoiding engagement and not learning to circle. Some trainers mistakenly shorten the longe line to gain more control only to then walk around on a small circle themselves in order to keep the horse's circle large. This will never keep the circle round and does not teach the horse to be independent. Always give or retract the longe line to change the size of the circle. Allow the horse to change his track by following whatever length of line you provide. You need to remain stationary in the center.

While arbitrarily shortening the side reins may appear to put the horse into a better working position, it actually teaches the opposite of what he needs to learn. He will lean into the rein because it will be easier than changing his balance. Shortening the side reins in slight increments allows the horse to relax and find that giving into the pressure is the better response. This is the way to lightness.

The horse should understand all the basic longe commands and circle comfortably before the side reins are connected. Keep in mind that longe training should overlap other in-hand lessons as well as riding in the Phase I position. This means that the horse should already flex the jaw to tension in the rein and readily release down into the lengthened position. Begin by connecting the side reins so they are long enough that no contact with the bit is possible, even with the neck extended. The horse will merely feel the weight of the rein. Shorten the rein only in conjunction with the horse's willingness to flex the jaw and bring the nose in—the rein should not demand flexion.

Shorten the side reins one notch at a time, keeping both sides the same length. The time between incremental changes will depend on the horse's ability to relax and reposition. Be willing to lengthen the rein whenever the horse stresses over tension in the rein. Stay on the side of caution—there is no harm in shortening the side reins very slowly. The goal is to shorten the reins until the horse's forehead is al-

most vertical, with the neck just above level with the withers. In this position the horse's head will come to vertical as he releases to tension in the rein. The horse's neck may shift up and down while he is developing better balance, but the neck should stabilize at slightly above the level of the withers once the horse gains comfort in a working position.

As the side reins are shortened, the horse may want to step backward. This is a natural response. If this happens, allow the horse to move. Finding how to release the pressure on the bit is a learning process. Allow the horse to move and stop without help or force.

Once the horse is confirmed on the longe, it is acceptable to adjust the inside side rein one

Longeing without the side reins connected allows the horse to acclimate to the feeling of the gear and any jingling sounds it may make.

notch shorter than the outside rein (by this time the horse should also work with good length bend under saddle). Shortening the inside rein confirms the already established bend.

There should be no possible restraint with the first connection of the side reins. The horse feels only the weight of the rein as it hangs loosely.

The goal of side reins is to position the head in front of vertical so that when the horse relaxes his jaw, he comes to vertical with slack in the reins. Shortening the side reins more brings the horse behind the vertical when he releases tension.

The horse will confront tension in the side rein as he learns the release. Once he relaxes into a near-vertical position, there should be slack in the reins.

Using a longeing caveson ensures that the line doesn't interfere with the side reins. Overcheck reins (optional for most horses) run along the horse's neck to keep his head from dropping too low.

Continuously longeing with the neck lower than the withers places too much emphasis on the shoulders. Although riding in the Phase I position gives preference to the lower position, the rider can direct the horse off his shoulder. On the longe the trainer lacks this level of control. Allowing the horse to be continuously on his shoulder will disconnect his haunch. You should expect the horse to drop his head from time to time. It is only a concern when he continues to favor a very low neck carriage. Then, overcheck reins can be used to prevent this behavior.

Fanny shows relaxation on the longe by tracking freely and in balance on the circle. The slack in both the side reins and the longe line reflects the correctness of her movement.

Once the horse circles correctly on the longe, moving the longe circle within the manège adds new dimension to the training process. When the trainer steps forward to walk parallel to the wall, with the horse in motion, she advances the position of the longe circle. By taking

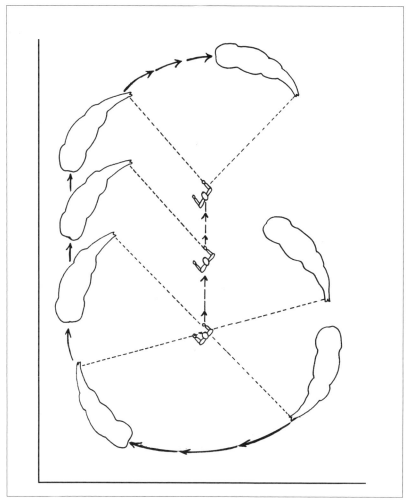

Shoulders-in on the longe. This diagram demonstrates the correct way of moving the circle within the manège. The trainer should stay the same distance from the wall.

Never hook the longe line directly onto the bit. I've seen every imaginable method of going up, down, around and through, and under and over. It doesn't matter how you configure it, because none of these connections will work in this teaching system. The goal is no resistance: The longe line is not intended to function with the same degree of softness as the rein. You can't teach lightness if you pull or hold tension on the bit in any fashion. If you don't have a caveson, the halter ring is the next best option.

two strides forward as the horse circles from the wall, the horse's shoulder will follow the longe line, producing a shoulders-in movement. After taking the two strides, the trainer stops so the horse returns to a round circle.

The head and neck position obtained through longe training should carry over into training under saddle. For many horses this carriage establishes a correct working position. For the dressage horse, it forms the base from which engagement and riding through the bit develop.

FREE LONGEING

Within the context of teaching lightness, the purpose of free longeing is to further help the horse understand balance. The use of a round pen is highly recommended, although some of the lessons in balance may be better delivered in the full manège where the horse corners, straightens, and has more room to adjust his stride.

The basic principles of longeing also apply to working free. The more the horse adheres to the aids on the longe, the more likely he is to listen when free. To avoid unnecessary confusion, wait until longe work is fluid with the side reins connected.

To free longe in the full manège, the trainer needs the help of one or two assistants. Each participant should carry a longe whip. Accordingly, the lead trainer stands in the center with an assistant at one or both ends. The combination of position, body language, and the direction of the whip is what will move the horse around the manège. The horse can be asked to circle in any size, make a figure eight, or stay along the wall. Constantly changing the path teaches the horse how to adjust stride and balance at any gait.

Free longeing disciplines the horse to pay full attention to the trainer. In return he is empowered to think and make decisions. Young horses tend to adapt to this freedom faster than seasoned horses, who may have become reliant on direct aids. Nevertheless, free longeing is a useful way to develop the horse's ability to think and take responsibility. Horses of any age and background should work free at some period during training. We recommend that readers learn more about the particulars of free longeing and round pen training before integrating these methods into their training programs.

CHAPTER 7

Body Mechanics of Horse and Rider

The horse's back should feel like a gentle river moving softly beneath the rider—relaxation allows the spine to flow with energy.

Understanding how the horse uses his body to balance his own movement gives the rider insight into the technical correctness of academic training. Balance and technical correctness coincide in every exercise. For example, the horse's legs can track in a shoulders-in way without proper length bend (spinal alignment) for the movement. Continuing to practice the exercise with poor body position may build strength and improve delivery, but, because the horse and rider are not technically correct, they will be unable achieve real lightness. Without the correct length bend and disposition of the back, shoulders-in, or any movement for that matter, cannot flow forward freely and will not gymnasticize the horse effectively. Mastering the basic exercise positions ensures technical correctness in all the horse does. Academic movement should become second nature. Only then will practice mature each exercise properly.

ALIGNMENT OF THE SPINE

The spine contains the nerves that transport messages throughout the horse's body. A good connection from the brain (thought) to the hind end (motor) increases the horse's ability to respond. The muscles on each side of the spinal column need to be in top physical condition to provide the strength to carry out that response.

The proper alignment of the spine starts with flexibility at the poll and in the neck. Earlier chapters discussed how relaxing the jaw prompts the horse to flex the poll at the first cervical vertebra (for front-to-back head movement) and then at the second cervical vertebra (for side-to-side head movement). This is why suppling should start at the front of the horse and work backward to the tail. Achieving alignment along the entire length of the spine enables all of the muscles to gymnasticize in an advantageous sequence.

THE NECK

The neck needs to be correctly aligned to the shoulder to allow energy to efficiently flow foward. Overbending the neck from side to side can misalign the spine laterally. This is counterproductive when teaching lightness because it causes a disjunction between the neck and the shoulder—the horse can avoid flexing the body, thus evading full engagement. Softness and flexibility of the neck come as a result of flexing or articulating the rib cage.

Flexing the neck behind the second cervical vertebra (most commonly at the fourth) also misaligns the spine. This "kink," as it is called, can be avoided by allowing the horse to stretch down and work in a long and low frame. Ample time working in Phase I is necessary to encourage the hind legs to track well forward with unrestricted freedom of movement. If the rider prematurely brings the head to vertical, usually by overshortening the rein, the neck lifts and shortens before the horse's body has been sufficiently conditioned to carry the position. This changes the dynamics of energy flow through the neck and positions the spine in such a way that most horses can't then use their back with optimum effectiveness.

THE BACK

Utilization of the back is fundamental to the horse's overall physical strength, fitness, and ability to engage. The horse's back is the key to achieving the efficiency of energy needed to reach a higher level of lightness. A true partnership between horse and rider depends on the rider's sensitivity to the movement of horse's back and her ability to interpret and respond to what she feels from his body as a whole. Academic balance (for almost all modern exercises) places the center

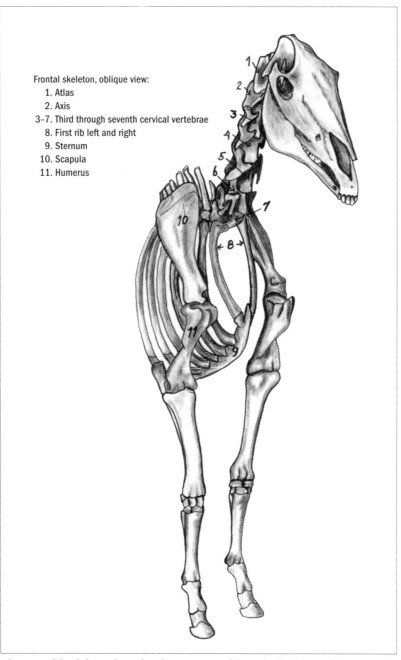

Frontal skeleton, oblique view:
1. Atlas
2. Axis
3–7. Third through seventh cervical vertebrae
8. First rib left and right
9. Sternum
10. Scapula
11. Humerus

This view of the skeleton shows that the connection of the neck, shoulder, and chest is purely muscular—there is no bony connection. Beginning at the hyoid bones of the TMJ, the sterohyoideus muscle connects to the sternum and the omohyoideus muscle connects to the shoulder. These muscular connections form a direct link between the horse's tongue and the lower neck, shoulder, and chest. With tension in the sternum, the horse cannot attain optimal bend over his top line or fully engage.

of balance beneath the rider's seat. To achieve this balance, the back must flex from side to side and up and down while holding the weight of the horse's body and carrying the weight of the rider.

Most average horses cannot round the back until suppled laterally first. By first stretching to relax the spine, then flexing laterally to supple (thereby stimulating even more relaxation), the horse is positioned to develop the strength necessary to round his back upward. When schooled properly, the direct connection between the poll and the haunch is maintained through longitudinal bend. Eventually, this connects the outside rein to the inside hind leg. The back is the critical conduit that holds the connection together (first laterally, then longitudinally).

If the back isn't strong enough to hold the bend, the horse can't sink the hip to achieve deep engagement. It is the process of working through each training exercise, in the order of difficulty, that gymnasticizes (supples and strengthens) the back for the highest level of functionality. The back and ribs gymnasticize through length bend on the circle and in all lateral work. As the rider's inside leg asks the horse to bend, the horse's spine and ribs "fill-up," or articulate outward, underneath the rider's outside leg and outside seat bone. This development is what strengthens the horse to lift the rider.

The back strengthens through spinal alignment, development of the haunch, and then gradually through more strenuous engagement. To help develop this full functionality, the rider must be aware of the disposition of the horse's back at all times. The back can be in one of these three positions:

- The back is raised and the horse is engaged (in accordance with his capabilities at that time).
- The back is neutral.
- The back is dropped or hollowed out.

Many movements require the horse to work in the raised position. However, much of the time the back can be neutral (and still support the rider) but capable of rounding when required. Problems occur when the back dips down. This can happen directly behind the withers, giving the rider a subtle loss of solidness or power. Also, it can happen from the loin forward, rendering the horse's entire back hollow. In either case, the result is the same: The back doesn't support the rider. Full energy from the haunch is blocked from forward movement, and impulsion dissipates into the body's tissue. Not enough power will reach the front end to consider the horse fully, or even sufficiently, engaged.

Conditioning and strengthening the horse adequately before moving on to more difficult exercises is simply common sense. Nevertheless, setbacks are inevitable. Fatigue often causes the horse to drop his back behind the withers. If this occurs, continue strengthening the horse using transitions, circles, and lateral work.

If the back hollows from the loin/sacral area, the problem may be more difficult to diagnose and overcome. The trouble may still be a lack of strength and fitness, but the sacroiliac joint can be a source of weakness. The sacral area lies beneath the loin where the flat plate of fused lumbar vertebrae (at the end of the spine) connects to the ilium, the large bone of the pelvis. The longissimus dorsi muscles lie along each side the vertebrae from the poll to the sacral area. The strength of these muscles allows the spine to articulate laterally while also holding longitudinal bend. The same muscles support the static position of the lumbar vertebrae as the back rises.

Although the static position of the spine in the sacral area is one of strength, inherent weakness may surface as training teaches the horse to tilt the pelvis backward. The pelvis should tilt when the haunch fully engages. Some horses may have avoided this level of engagement in the past. Be aware that pushing the horse into mobilizing the haunch too quickly can produce soreness in the back. It may also reveal an existing problem unnoticed under less strenuous engagement.

Pain or weakness in the hind legs may also manifest as weakness in the back before any visible lameness in the leg. By overcompensating on the "good" leg, the horse can stress the fused position of the sacrum (lumbar vertebrae). Although the sacroiliac articulates as a whole unit (as the haunch lowers), stress or movement within the joint itself results in weakness and pain to the back.

Most horses will gymnasticize through training without ever drawing attention to the back. Furthermore, most of the horses that do show signs weakness will strengthen through continued exercise. The purpose of this discussion is to heighten the rider's awareness to what can occur. Whenever problems persist or do not appear to improve, call for a medical analysis to determine the root of the condition.

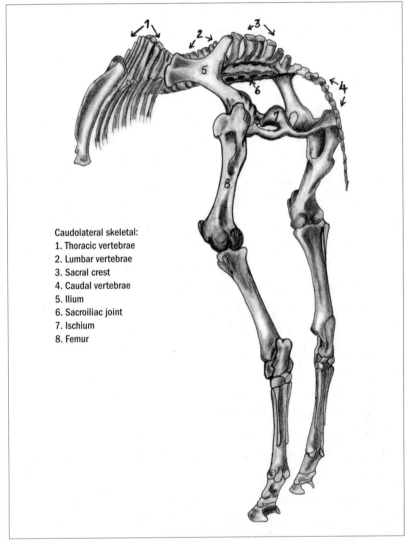

Caudolateral skeletal:
1. Thoracic vertebrae
2. Lumbar vertebrae
3. Sacral crest
4. Caudal vertebrae
5. Ilium
6. Sacroiliac joint
7. Ischium
8. Femur

This skeletal view shows how the articulation of the thoracic vertebrae forms length bend. It also shows that the static condition of the lumbar vertebrae and the sacrum cannot participate in the horse's lateral bend. Instead, by tilting to the rear and down, the lumbar rotates the pelvis, allowing the horse's hind legs to track beneath him in a position of strength. This permits full engagement of the haunch and supports the back in longitudinal bend.

THE HAUNCH

The alignment of the spine is essential for optimal engagement of the hind end. The role of the haunch is to sink and lift the back into longitudinal bend. Deep engagement—tracking the hind legs forward, well under the body to support the horse's shift in weight and balance to a position beneath the rider—requires considerable strength in the haunch.

CONFORMATION

Familiarity with the mechanics of the neck, back, and haunch helps the rider understand technical correctness in academic training, but conformation can also affect performance.

Here are some attributes to look for in the horse:

- A clean, open throatlatch gives the horse room to flex comfortably at C1 and C2 and also provides good air passage.
- A neck that attaches higher on the chest allows the horse to be lighter on the forehand.
- A wide chest, with the front legs outside the chest box, allows greater lateral reach.
- The optimal length of the horse is 1/3 neck, 1/3 back, and 1/3 haunch.
- Look for withers that are level or slightly higher than the haunch.
- A shorter top line and longer bottom line equates to solid athletic ability.
- A deep heart girth indicates good lung capacity.
- The shoulder angle should be well sloping and equal to the angle of the hip.
- Broad width across the loin indicates a strong back.
- The front legs should be straight.
- The hind legs should track out a few degrees from the stifle to avoid clipping the front heels when tracking deeply.
- A large round hoof will support the horse.

While each of these attributes is valuable, not all are necessary, nor is it realistic to expect to find them all in one horse. But they are useful for assessing a horse's athletic potential. The ability of the rider will inevitably control how well the horse advances and performs. A competent rider can take an intelligent horse with just average conformation to advanced levels of performance in almost any discipline.

THE POSITION OF THE RIDER

Remember the fundamentals of riding in lightness:

- When the horse is relaxed, supple, and strong, his energy flows freely forward with such intensity that he is able to be light to the aids without any driving force from the rider.
- When the horse has the strength to balance himself, the rider has no need to hold tension in the rein. The balance lies within the horse.

When I get up on someone's horse for the first time, they don't understand the immediate difference in the way their horse moves. I haven't taught anything—I simply mounted up and began to ride. What people see is their horse's response to my relaxation. If you relax, your horse will thank you in much the same way.

While the quandary over which came first, the chicken or the egg, may remain unsolved, there is no question that the rider must be balanced in her seat in order to educate the horse to find his balance. The entire training process consists of exercises that develop, maintain—or regain—balance. Don't expect the horse to stay in balance if he must continually compensate for an unbalanced rider.

Furthermore, it is the rider's relaxation, as much as the horse's, that enables the horse to progress in lightness. The degree of relaxation required of the rider is admittedly great when pursuing lightness: The horse can't obtain true impulsion without the relaxation of the rider. It is the rider's responsibility not to block or inhibit his forward movement.

The priority of this book is to teach the horse how to relax. While the rider's relaxation is similarly promoted, it is assumed that she comes to the program able to ride in a balanced position. If she trusts the concept of lightness and commits to relaxation, she will learn the art of this system and feel the freedom of riding in lightness.

Relaxation is not being limp—it's being soft, responsive, and giving. It means the rider accepts the horse's release to the aids and allows his energy to flow through her body as well. It's not easy for riders who have been accustomed to reaching for the rein or driving with the leg to all of a sudden let go of these impulses. It takes time to become as light and as sensitive as this system requires.

The following points will help the rider improve a relaxed and balanced position:

- **Head up.** This helps the rider to stay balanced through the shoulders. When training, there is a tendency to look down at the horse's shoulders. Looking down tilts the head forward, creating tension in the shoulders. Hold the head as if suspended by a cord from above.

- **Resist pulling the rein.** Never doubt that a pulling hand positions the horse to resist. It is a fixed hand that teaches the horse to look for a way out.

- **Secure the rein with the thumb.** If the rein is secured through the tightening of fingers, the whole arm tightens, creating tension.

- **Quiet hands.** The quieter the hands are, the more the horse can feel lightness.

- **Direct the horse from the shoulders, seat, and leg.** Become less and less dependent on the rein as the horse's training advances. Where the rider's seat and body goes, the horse will follow.

- **Relax the shoulders.** Rigidity in the rider's shoulders makes it more difficult for the horse to utilize his back. Instead, relax the shoulders and release them downward towards the hips. This keeps the upper body balanced and moving with the horse.

- **Relax the elbows close to the body.** When the waist rotates, it rotates the shoulders and arms, therefore adjusting the rein. For a schooled horse, this slight movement in the rein is all that is necessary to communicate an aid.

- **Balance the horse directly under the seat.** The old masters balanced the horse behind the seat, primarily for such exercises as *courbette* and airs like *croupade*. This is not practical for today's rider, with the exception of some advanced movements outside the scope of this book.

Do you pull on the reins when you ride? Test your answer the next time you ride. Count the number of times you pull back on the rein, for any reason. You may be surprised. Use the fixed rein instead of pulling, and your ride will improve (see Phase I: Beginning the Circle).

- **Move the waist like a ball bearing.** Rolling with the horse's movement allows the rider's seat to absorb energy from the horse without constricting his forward motion. Failure to move with the horse blocks, or at least impedes, the free flow of energy.

- **The rider's legs should hang like pendulums.** Relax the leg right from the hip. Gripping with the legs affects the horse's breathing and tightens his back. It diminishes both the rider's and the horse's ability to feel. The way to enhance feeling is through relaxation. Only apply leg pressure if it is needed.

- **Relax the knee.** This allows the rider to use the lower leg effectively.

- **Raise the toe.** Don't try to push the heel down; instead, think about raising the toe. This allows the inside and backside of the leg to relax.

- **Apply the aids only when and where needed.** Riding with relaxation and lightness means teaching the horse and then getting out of the way.

Analyzing the rider's position in its entirety can make problems seem insurmountable, when in reality just a few adjustments can make a lot of difference for success. Examining the riding position piece by piece may help in evaluating weaknesses and make improvements.

Remember, it's a lack of attention that allows bad habits to form. Being aware of your weaknesses, on the other hand, will allow you to focus on improvement.

CHAPTER 8

Tack and Accessories

Teaching is not about tack. If the rider relies on gadgets to commu-
nicate with the horse, both the rider and the horse miss something
in the translation.

The proper fit and correct use of riding equipment is important in all equestrian disciplines. Because the principles of riding in lightness cross discipline lines, the style of saddle or bridle is immaterial in this training program. A brief discussion about fitting equipment to the horse is in order, however, and identifying other tack and accessories may be helpful to the process of training the horse to be light to the aids. The basis for this discussion is that lightness aspires to a heightened degree of communication, and, accordingly, faulty or poorly fitting equipment interferes with the effective delivery of the aids.

THE BIT

A simple jointed snaffle is my bit of choice for training in any riding discipline because the position of the joint in the middle of the mouth encourages the horse to lift and savor the bit. By design, snaffle bits work on the corners of the horse's mouth. Having the reins connect at the corners of the mouth promotes flexion and lateral bend.

Selecting a snaffle needn't be a mystery. Correct fit is the most important factor. The width of the bit should just reach to the corners of the horse's lip. A snaffle with a fixed-ring is preferable to a loose-ring snaffle. In this category the full-cheek snaffle offers the most advantages: Not only will it stop the bit from sliding through the horse's mouth, which is important when teaching a response to an opening rein, but it also addresses the often-overlooked fact that flexion begins by drawing the horse into bend from the opposing side. As the inside rein initiates direction, the outside ring of the bit supports the movement. The full-cheek simply covers more surface area on the outside of the mouth than other snaffles, and thus it assists in guiding the flexion process. The stability of the full-cheek continues to serve a good purpose throughout the training process, although some advanced horses respond well to a Baucher snaffle. The advantages gained by using a loose-ring bit are in the province of the advanced rider and are outside the scope of this book.

The headstall should be adjusted so that the bit just meets the corner of the horse's mouth, without creating any wrinkles. This looser-than-usual fit requires the horse to hold the bit in place with his tongue and also gives him room to lift and savor the bit.

When purchasing a bit, high-quality products are likely to have smooth surfaces and be balanced on each side of the mouthpiece. While steel makes a good bit component, horses like the taste of copper in their mouths. Because a solid copper mouthpiece can produce too much acidity in the saliva, a combination of the two metals makes a wise choice. If you're participating in competition, be sure to verify that the bit you are using is acceptable.

The diameter of the snaffle depends upon the conformation of the horse's mouth. A thinner bit is recommended for a horse that has a fleshy tongue and thick jawbone. If these features are refined, a thicker mouthpiece will provide more comfort. The size of the mouthpiece—whether thick or thin—does not necessarily equate to severity. Teaching the horse to release to the slightest pressure makes the design of the bit in general a lesser consideration.

Most horses work well in a plain jointed snaffle. Starting with a basic bit allows the horse to learn to hold the mouthpiece without distraction. Some high-strung horses, however, may like a bit with a movable center piece to slide or roll on their tongue. It may help them dissipate nervous energy. This is very individualized—consider a specialty bit only if it enables the horse to offer more relaxation.

The horse can ride in the same snaffle throughout training and thereafter. There is no mandate to change bits, unless precluded by rules of competition. Many horses, however, will at some point move to a shank bit. Connecting the rein to a shank changes the horse's alignment. The rein connection at the end of the shank lowers the horse's head and neck carriage. The addition of leverage through a chin strap sharpens the horse's response.

When the horse has learned to release to pressure in a snaffle, switching to a shank bit can be accomplished with minimal adjustment. Begin using the new bit by working in hand. Next, ride several sessions without attaching the curb strap or chain. Then attach the strap or chain loosely, so there is no chance of pinching the lip. Refine the adjustment over several rides. Always leave enough slack in the curb rein to allow the horse time to respond to the rein aid before feeling leverage on the jaw from the curb strap or chain.

Remember, most bits are not deemed severe as long as the rider doesn't pull the rein. Conversely, any disrespect through the hand will be threatening to the horse, regardless of the bit used.

THE BRIDLE

Any type of headstall can hold the bit in place. Throughout training, however, the noseband or caveson should either be removed or buckled so loosely that the horse won't feel it's there. The horse needs free mobility of the jaw in order to relax, lift, and savor the bit. Otherwise, tightening the noseband inhibits this necessary movement.

This horse's tension is evident as he gapes his mouth open. Tightening a noseband to close the mouth does nothing to change the underlying problem. A loose noseband will confine the excessive movement and place the horse in a position in which he can learn to relax.

Nosebands shouldn't play a big role in training, yet, when the horse opens his mouth, many riders tighten the strap in an attempt to keep the horse's mouth closed. Since no amount of tautness can shut the jaw completely, restraining movement only causes the horse to resist. Opening the mouth is usually learned behavior, generally as a consequence of being pulled by the rein. The horse's resistance to pulling results in habitual tension, and therefore pulling is contradictory to training in lightness. The horse's mouth should be quiet on the bit. Teaching relaxation and release of the jaw can overcome a mouth-opening problem, whereas tightening the noseband can only mask the bad conduct.

> When a horse gapes the jaw open to extreme, a noseband will be necessary to obtain the baseline position from which relaxation can be achieved. Buckle the caveson so two fingers can slide easily between the band and the jaw. This allows movement while stopping any excessive behavior.

Because riding in lightness precludes pulling the rein, there is no physical reason for the horse to open his mouth. Still, he may continue to act from habit. When allowed time to relax and adjust to the freedom of moving the jaw without being pulled, most horses will stop opening the mouth and simply release when feeling the rein aid.

THE SADDLE

Any type of saddle may be used during training. Proper fit to the horse's back conformation and comfort to the rider are the main requirements. Optimal performance depends upon full utilization of the horse's back—the all-important lift or rounding of the back won't

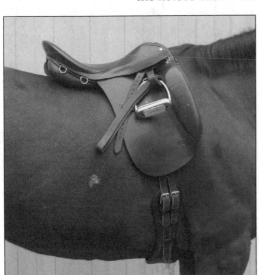

occur if the saddle presses or pinches the horse. With the weight of the rider in the saddle, adequate clearance over the withers is part of correct fit. The saddle's tree must be wide enough to span the withers and not pinch anywhere along the backbone. A wide saddle can be padded to fit a narrow horse.

Many riders position the saddle so the girth falls directly behind the horse's elbow. This places the saddle too far forward on the withers and interferes with the movement of the shoulder. It also tilts the rider back, resulting in an unbalanced position or requiring more padding under the saddle to balance the rider.

However, when the saddle is too narrow or contacts the withers, no amount of padding will make it an appropriate fit. Keep in mind that the horse's conformation changes with age and development. Saddle padding should be reviewed periodically.

The seat of the saddle should be level; the rider shouldn't feel that the saddle is tipping her forward or throwing her back as she moves with the stride of the horse. Judge the fit of the saddle by tacking the horse without padding. Check for ample clearance over the backbone and feel for any bridging between the contact points of the saddle and the horse's back. Obtain a professional opinion if you are concerned whether the saddle fits correctly.

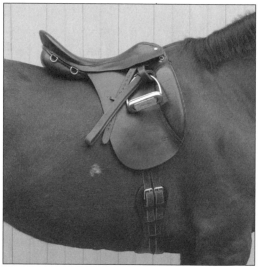

Placing the saddle well behind the withers gives the horse freedom in the shoulder and levels the saddle seat so the rider sits in a balanced position.

THE WHIP

The whip needs to be understood as an extension of the rider's arm or leg. The main purpose of the whip is to assist the rider in applying the aids where they will most help the horse to understand. At times the whip can be used to insist, but it is not a tool for discipline. The horse knows the difference between assistance and punishment. Riders hold the responsibility to be virtuous in their actions.

In order to be effective, the whip must reach to the haunch. A moderately stiff whip conveys positive energy. If the whip is too soft, it can sway with the horse's movement, causing the rider to make unintended contact. Dressage-style whips are suitable in length and maneuverability.

Application of the whip extends from the horse's shoulder and forearm, back to the flank, and up to the top of the rump. Desensitizing the horse to the whip is discussed in Working In Hand and in Longeing; the same guidelines apply under saddle. When horses are worked in hand with the whip, the transition to riding with the whip is usually minimal.

Begin with a single whip. Later on, try riding with a whip in each hand. This gives you the ability to respond quickly, providing assistance when and where it is needed. The academic benefit from the second whip doesn't come into play until the horse becomes fluid with lateral exercises.

THE SPUR

This tool is quite often misunderstood. The purpose of the spur is to help the horse elevate or move sideways; it is not meant to drive the horse forward. To effectively elevate the horse, the spur must touch below the ribs. (Shorter riders may need to position the spur lower on the heel of their boot to use it effectively.) When the spur is applied correctly, the horse lifts the rider with greater flexion.

Relative to the spur, the rider's heel covers a large area when it presses against the horse's side. The small diameter of the spur allows the rider to make precise touches that convey distinct meanings to the horse. Therefore, the rider's heel alone is unlikely to match the fine-tuning obtainable with the spur.

Spurs are most effective on sensitive horses. An advanced rider can use the spur to focus a reactive horse inward and onto the aids so that he is less distracted by extraneous stimuli. Lethargic horses—or ones that are dead to the side—respond better to the whip.

It is not necessary to add spurs while advancing through the lessons in this training program. The spur is a sophisticated aid requiring an accomplished and mature rider. No rider should wear a spur without knowing where the heel is at all times. If, however, the rider has confidence to apply the spur correctly, the horse's heightened awareness to the aids will benefit his performance. But before the horse can comprehend how to respond to the spur with upward lift, he must first understand both lateral and longitudinal bend. This means the rider can choose to introduce the spur toward the end of Phase II training, once the horse has both the ability to lift and the thought process to appreciate the intention of the aid.

Think of the spur as a progression from the whip. Moving to the spur follows from the rider's use of one or possibly two whips, to the inside spur alone, and finally to the addition of the outside spur. Once the horse rides to the spur, the rider should discontinue using the whip, first eliminating one then the other. The goal is for the horse to work almost exclusively from the rider's seat aids, allowing the rider's legs to hang pendulum-like at the horse's side. The spur touches the horse under the ribs to provide an activating spark as needed.

Preparation for the spur starts in hand. Touch the horse's side with the fingertips to convey the feeling of the spur. Then begin riding a *volte* with the spur to the inside. Delicately caress the horse's side (with on and off contact) to spiral the *volte* into a large circle. Add the second spur after the horse relaxes to the touch of the inside spur on each side.

Both horse and rider must be comfortable with the use of either the whip or spur as aids. These aids can be invaluable; however, if the rider lacks confidence or the ability to use the aids correctly, the result will stress both horse and rider. Relaxation is always the foremost factor. Many riders, including some that are advanced, are more successful using leg and heel aids alone.

BOOTS, WRAPS, AND HEEL PROTECTION

The horse's safety is always a concern. For training purposes, protective wraps are meant to guard against a hoof coming into contact with another leg. All horses, no matter how athletic, will hit themselves at some point during lateral training, so front split boots or wraps are recommended during this phase. (Correctly performed, the exercises in this book do not warrant extra support for the tendons, unless the horse has a preexisting condition.) Some horses will also need rear wraps or ankle boots. If the horse overreaches, bell boots will be necessary. The rider should make use of whatever protective equipment allows the horse to work safely. Any chronic interference should be discussed with a farrier and/or veterinarian.

DRAW REINS

The use of draw reins can play a limited but valuable role in teaching lightness. The term draw rein refers to a long rein that attaches to the girth at one end and runs through the ring of the bit to the rider's hand. Draw reins are not intended to replace the regular reins or speed up the normal process of teaching the horse to release the jaw and flex the poll. Some horses can be so reluctant to release, however, that the rider can't achieve a release with the regular rein; in such cases draw reins can perform a useful function—to show the horse that the flexed position can be agreeable. Draw reins allow the horse to feel enough security in his balance that he can begin to relax and release tension.

The softness that can be achieved with the draw rein will encourage the horse to make a change without the rider's need to apply any force.

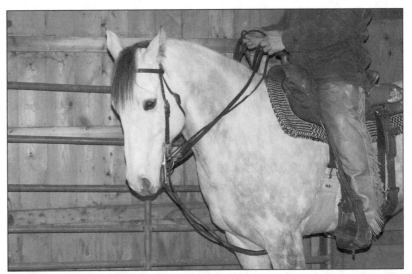

The limited use of draw reins can help horses that are having difficulty finding the release to the rein while in motion. If the horse isn't releasing through the back, it is best to run the draw reins between the front legs. This lower position shows the horse that he can stretch downward. Photo: Willis Steele

If the horse is unwilling to release at the poll, it is best to attach the draw reins to the sides of the girth. This position helps the horse release at the poll while going forward. Photo: Willis Steele

This makes the limited use of draw reins acceptable. Remember that any elasticity in the draw rein extends the duration of contact with the bit (see Longeing). The horse needs to release to pressure—elasticity blurs his understanding that a release will eliminate pressure. For this reason no type of stretchable rein or mechanical pulley system is advised.

RIDING WITH DRAW REINS

Using draw reins is only slightly different from using normal reins. The draw rein is used in conjunction with the regular rein, adjusting it slightly shorter than the regular rein. Begin by working the horse on a twenty-meter circle in the long-and-low position. Make contact with the inside draw rein only. The draw rein "draws" the horse's nose to the inside of the circle; simultaneously the rein draws the horse's nose down and back as he moves forward. When the rein aid is subtle, the horse is less likely to resist. Do not pull the horse into position; rather, allow the horse to follow the "draw" of the rein. By requesting only slight flexion, the horse is less likely to lose relaxation. (Initially, some tension may be exhibited. This is acceptable as long as the horse recovers quickly.) After making several flexes on the inside rein, change rein to supple the horse on the other inside rein.

Draw reins are most successful when used sparingly. Each session with draw reins should be followed by one or two sessions using the regular reins alone. Each time, follow the same inside rein exercise to test the horse's willingness to release to the regular rein. If he is reluctant, ride with draw reins again. Use this on and off approach until the horse relaxes and releases to the regular rein alone.

Remember, draw reins do not teach; they only position. While it is ideal for the horse to learn to release to the regular rein, using draw reins is appropriate when a horse exhibits little comprehension of flexation. For the best results, use draw reins to address a specific issue, then take them away. Since an apprehension to release can surface at any gait or at all gaits, draw reins may be used during different segments of training. But avoid prolonged periods of continuous usage—this risks dependency on the draw rein for position.

Keep in mind that the draw rein connection, however soft, causes the horse's response—he does not yet understand how to flex on his own. The intention is to minimize his stress so he stays relaxed. Pulling the draw rein forces a dramatic change of position. This can be overwhelming; instead of following his nose down, he may lift his head up, fighting against the rein and compressing his neck into an unnatural position.

CHAPTER 9

Phase 1:
Beginning the Circle

Don't try to make the horse something he's not. Allow him to be
comfortable "in his own skin."

Work on the circle is the essential building block for the horse's
gymnastic development and advancement. Circling creates
and maintains suppleness, then becomes the test of it. Longeing asked
the horse to form a circle and find some degree of balance without the
rider. The search for an "educated" balance continues, now under the
direction of the mounted rider.

Circles can have a reassuring effect on both horse and rider, providing a safe haven where they can find comfort in what they know.
Horses quickly acquire a feeling for safety, so it is prudent for the rider
to use the circle to the best possible advantage. The horse has no need
to rush because the circle goes nowhere but around. This soothing effect facilitates the release of tension from any training lesson: Issues
defuse and composure is regained (for both horse and rider) by returning to the sanctuary of the circle at any time.

Moving "straight on the circle" means the horse's body is holding
correct poll to croup length bend. Straightness, however, is complicated by the fact that the horse's hips are wider than his shoulders.
When left to his natural devices, the horse will align his shoulder to the
wall; consequently, his hips track to the inside, making him, in fact,
crooked. On a circle, however, bending around the rider's inside leg
causes the horse's inside hind leg to track slightly under his barrel and
toward the arc of the circle. The ribs push outward, creating the arc
called length bend. This arc in the horse's body aligns the shoulders

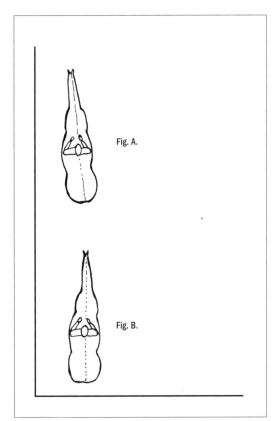

Fig. A.

Fig. B.

Straight to the wall. Fig. A. The horse will naturally align the shoulder to the wall. Because the haunch is wider than the shoulder, the horse will track crookedly. Fig. B. Riding straight to the wall means keeping the horse's spine parallel to the wall.

and the hips an equal distance from the "wall" of the circle, giving rise to the phrase "straight on the circle."

Length bend increases as the diameter of the circle decreases. Therefore, when beginning work on the circle, the horse needs to be guided by the aids to find the correct bend for each size circle. Circles compel the horse to listen to the aids when there are no walls for guidance or protection. The rider applies the aids when the horse needs assistance and allows the horse to move forward when he is correct. This develops both the horse's understanding of the aids and his own understanding of bend. Without this experience, the horse will expect the rider to do all the thinking, which contradicts the goal of cohesive teamwork.

Some horses will need time to track properly. When tracking in length bend, the horse's inside hind leg carries proportionately more weight than it does without bend. To compensate, the horse may drop his shoulder to the inside of the arc (less commonly to the outside), or he might push the haunch in or out. Nevertheless, if the front end tracks well—meaning that the shoulders stay level on the circle—the rider can be less critical of how the hind end tracks. Unless the haunch is drastically out of alignment, further suppling will encourage the haunch to follow the arc of the bend.

Circles include spirals, serpentines, and figure eights. Changing the degree of bend as the size of the circle changes, or changing the direction of bend on a serpentine line or on a figure eight, are all part of the dynamics called "circle training." Train with variety: change rein frequently, change the size of the circle, and change the position of the circle within the manège. Change is the key to developing flexibility.

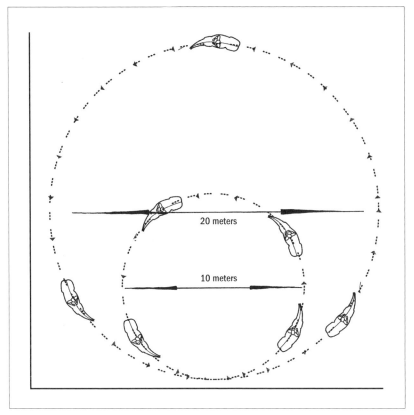

Straight on the circle. The horse's length bend conforms to the arc of the circle. Illustration: Cecily L. Steele

Suppleness and flexibility are developed through bending, not by holding bend.

When the rider begins to circle, the horse is asked to follow the inside opening rein with his nose. Once he is following the inside rein, the rider teaches the horse to bend around her inside leg. This progression is in accord with the fundamental concept of training front to back in order to ultimately ride back to front.

CIRCLE TRAINING

Start on a twenty-meter circle. A circle of this size will create definite length bend without overburdening the novice horse. As a rule the size of the circle on which the horse can effectively begin correct length bend depends on the horse's size and athletic ability. A green fifteen-hand horse will handle a small circle more easily than a green seventeen-hand horse, although this advantage diminishes with training.

Using the correct aids for the circle is essential. The rider's inside rein directs the horse to follow his nose, while her inside leg at the girth creates bend through the ribs and spine. By maintaining light support with the outside rein and resting her outside leg behind the girth, the rider supports forward movement with bend. Additionally, by aligning her shoulders to the horse's shoulders and her hips to the horse's hips, the rider begins to teach the horse to align his body to hers. (The ability to follow the rider's body takes time to develop.)

It is the horse's response to the aids that creates lightness. While the horse needs time to develop the skill to interpret the movement of the rider's body, the rein aids can be well defined from the beginning. There are four kinds of connection through the rein: a giving rein, a soft rein, a fixed rein, and a free rein.

The giving rein. The rider releases the rein forward by advancing her arm and/or allowing the rein to slide longer. The hand can maintain contact with the bit but allows no tension in the rein. The giving rein is the primary rein position used in Phase I. It is used to lengthen the horse down or whenever the horse leans on the rein.

The soft rein. With the rein between her thumb and first finger, the rider holds the rein at a fixed length. She makes soft contact with the bit by flexing her wrist or squeezing her fingers to create a slight draw/release motion. The length of the rein should be such that the horse will feel any vibration in the rein but not feel prolonged contact, which would compress his forward motion. The soft rein is the working rein of Phase II.

The fixed rein. The rider holds a solid connection to the bit. There is no pulling, although the rein may be shortened in order to make the solid connection possible. The fixed rein is used to make a statement. The horse must give to the solid connection and maintain the released position until the fixed rein softens. (See Phase II: Building a Working Frame.)

The free rein. The rider holds the rein at the buckle. The free rein is used to lengthen the horse down (although the rider will not always lengthen all the way to the buckle) or during breaks in schooling. The rider maintains some lateral guidance by using an opening rein, but no direct connection to the bit is practical at such a long length.

The degree of lightness required in the rein extends to all the rider's aids. Learning to ride and train in lightness requires the rider to relax tension. The horse will not attune to the rider's leg if the leg constantly presses. Likewise, if the rider sits heavily in the saddle, the horse won't be able to distinguish the seat aids.

Other riding methods tell the horse to wait to be driven forward by the rider. In contrast, riding in lightness requires the horse to learn to go forward without force. To effectively "drive" himself, the horse must feel freedom to move his energy forward. This means eliminating energy blocks from within the horse's body and also from within the rider's body. Nothing should impede the horse's impulsion. Both horse and rider must relax in order to unleash this level of freedom.

Any rider who hasn't experienced a horse trained in lightness may have difficulty imagining just how soft they are. Even so, the rider shouldn't expect to achieve lightness at the start of training. The aids grow more delicate over time. Some aids even change completely. For example: The inside rein plays an active role in teaching the circle. It is the inside rein that asks the horse to follow his nose and learn to bend around the rider's inside leg. Ultimately, the horse will bend around the rider's inside leg to the extent that the outside rein allows.

The rein and the leg are the first nonverbal aids to be taught, but as the rider trains, seat aids—the act of shifting weight—the use of the whip, and possibly the spur are all introduced to help the horse take direction. The horse learns from all these different sources. As the horse becomes more advanced, there should be less reliance on the

When I begin to work with a new student, one of the first things I tell them to do is relax. When I walk over and lift his or her calf away from the horse's side, I often find a leg that is wrapped tightly to the horse. I'll ask them again to relax, and the response is usually the same: "I am relaxed." Because most riders believe they must use force against the horse, their perception of relaxation is undeveloped. It takes time to understand what can be accomplished once you learn how to truly relax.

leg for impulsion and less dependence on the rein for direction. The seat and body replace the more obvious leg and rein aids as the aids evolve. Exercises on the circle begin this progression by teaching the horse awareness to the aids.

For the rider the first real test is maintaining the roundness of the circle through length bend. As in longeing, a round circle is essential. Little is gained by describing egg shapes or angles. The horse's suppleness and strength is only achieved through the fluidity of a consistent arc. The horse can't learn the lessons of the circle unless he is ridden correctly.

Riding in lightness assumes that horse and rider are partners. When the rider leads the partnership correctly, she trusts the horse to become thoughtful and capable of making good choices. The rider constantly offers an aid then allows the horse to find the right response.

While the horse is working on the longe and in hand, the trainer/ rider spends a lot of time observing movement and learning the natural timing of the different gaits. Under saddle the rider has more influence over the horse's way of going. Be mindful not to create or build upon false or unnatural movement. Don't push the horse outside his comfort zone. It can't be stressed enough that training in lightness does not force. It allows the horse time to build a solid, broad baseline of knowledge from which advancement can develop. Phases I and II serve to attain that base. The overarching concept is that when the base is broad, each individual movement is just a small modification of what the horse already comprehends and can perform.

Remaining within the horse's natural realm doesn't mean that his movement can't be enhanced. Riding correct circles in combination with the gymnastic benefits of lateral work will define the horse's gait academically and bring it to a higher level of elegance and sophistication.

RELAXING THE JAW

Riding the circle begins in the same way as the horse started in hand: The rider relaxes the jaw and lengthens the horse down. These are the defining principles of Phase I. Under saddle the rider's application of lightness in the rein can feel quite different from working in hand. It

Maintaining length bend is the first opportunity to delegate responsibility to the horse. Once the horse understands the aids for length bend, the rider should expect him to maintain the roundness of a circle. This expectation relies on you to ride the circle correctly. Become proficient at recognizing the correct bend for each circle size. Be able to judge diameters. Then ride the circle by riding the bend, not by using the rein.

may also be quite different from how the rider has handled the rein in the past. The horse's training depends on the rider's self-discipline to relax and be light.

Remember, in artistic equitation the concept of "forward" is unique: The horse steps "through" the hand and seat without resistance. Used in this way, "through" means free or continuous passage. This is completely different from the practice of "driving" the horse "into" the hand. The ultimate outcome may be similar, but conceptually the horse becomes lighter by stepping "through" rather than by stepping "into" a braced hand.

Riding the Exercise

Allow the horse to move freely forward with little contact in the rein. Vibrate the inside rein to relax the jaw, then flex the horse's nose to the inside. Once the horse releases through C1 and C2, the rider lengthens the rein to send the horse's head and neck down to stretch the muscles along the spine.

LENGTHENING DOWN

Bend is defined in two ways: as length or lateral bend from the nose to the tail along the side of the horse and as longitudinal bend over the top line from head to tail. Lengthening the horse down is a prerequisite to longitudinal bend The horse should ride in a long, stretched frame before being asked to ride through the bit or to build strength.

Riding the Exercise

Begin by walking on a twenty-meter circle. Vibrate the inside rein to relax the horse's jaw. Next, flex the nose to the inside by rotating the wrist on the inside hand so that the palm faces up and lifts the rein slightly higher. Then release both reins to send the horse's head down.

It is important to maintain the horse's forward motion on the circle. To do this, the rider rests her inside leg at the girth and her outside leg just behind the girth. She can use on and off pressure with the legs if the horse needs more impulsion. The goal is to stretch the head down, as low as it will go, while the horse steps actively forward.

The horse's release at C2 is confirmation that the jaw is relaxed. If the horse flexes the poll before relaxing the jaw, then there is no natural motivation for him to relax the jaw—he can merely set his head position without relaxation.

The combination of rotating and lifting the hand brings the nose to the inside. As the horse flexes, immediately release both reins to send his head and neck down. Stretching down is the horse's natural response. Do not impede the horse's stretch with any tension in the rein. I use smooth reins to insure that they slip smoothly through my fingers. Even lacing or webbing on the rein can impede the motion.

The photo shows the use of the inside rein to flex the horse to the inside. The outside rein then lifts upward into the corner of the horse's mouth to request a release to the rein.

The photo of the next stride shows the resulting downward release, which brings the horse through his back, pelvis, and neck. The horse can now use the hind end more effectively. Work in hand is a prerequisite for making this release.

Horses that have been taught this exercise in hand usually respond quickly to the aids under saddle, though some young or soft-backed horses may have difficulty accessing the back muscles. By sitting lightly, the rider facilitates the process for the horse. Lightly brushing the inside leg forward at the girth and lowering the hands will also encourage the horse's nose to the inside and then down. The rider can also lengthen the horse's head down while standing at a halt, then depart into a walk already in the lower frame.

Be aware that sitting lightly on the horse's back doesn't mean leaning forward. Shifting forward will encourage the horse to balance on the forehand. The rider needs to maintain a balanced riding position. Merely shifting some weight from the seat to the balls of the feet will ease weight off the saddle and relieve pressure on the horse's back.

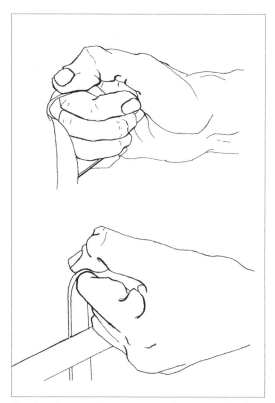

Hands in the normal rein position. Illustration: Cecily L. Steele

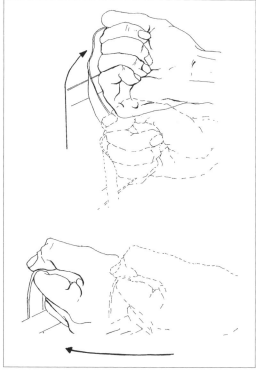

One hand rotates the wrist up to bend the horse as the other hand moves forward to encourage the horse's movement. Illustration: Cecily L. Steele

The Phase I position allows the horse to stretch down and relax his entire top line.

Begin riding the circle at the walk and trot only. You just want the horse to relax to the freedom from the rein and the rider's seat. Lift out the saddle to be light on his back. The rider should not sit the trot or use a pressing seat aid until the horse's back feels strong beneath the saddle. In all the gaits, lift off the back until the horse can relax and stretch while holding weight in the saddle.

THE PHASE I FRAME

The rider's goal in Phase I is to maintain the lowered position. Stay on the circle and begin with the walk and trot; later add the canter. The horse's nose should be at his knee level, bringing the neck below horizontal. Each time the horse brings his head up, use the aids to send it back down.

The horse must move forward freely. When the spine is stretched, unrestrained movement stretches all the muscles throughout the horse's body. The only contact with the bit should be in the initial vibration of the rein to relax the jaw. While correct shaping of the circle is of the utmost importance for training, the horse must first learn to lengthen down and follow his nose. Therefore, during the first few rides, don't be overly concerned about the roundness of the circle or the correctness of the gait. First establish freeness of movement. Let the circle, not the rein, control the horse's speed.

As the horse moves around the circle, his head and neck will rise to his own comfort level. The rider will need to repeatedly send him back down. As stretching spreads relaxation through his body, the horse should voluntarily maintain the lowered position. Once this happens, the riders can focus on the correct shape of the circle and the horse's rhythm.

This lowered position becomes the working frame for the horse in Phase I. Some horse and rider teams will achieve this lengthened-down position in a few rides, while others may take several weeks to become fluid with the movement. Nonetheless, do not stress over how long it takes.

Most of the Phase I work should be accomplished on the circle. For this reason, it is important that the work not become monotonous. The proactive rider will be responsive to success: Once the horse does something well, do something different even if it is only changing rein. Ride spirals and serpentines, and change the direction and position of the circle often.

Phase I challenges the rider to create lightness. Little contact with the bit is necessary. Allow the horse to carry his natural pace freely, and resist the urge to influence his movement. The rider can make light contact with the rein but should not compress or confine the forwardness of the gait. Allow the horse to find his own balance for the frame.

Some riders will instinctively look to the rein and seat to take "control" of the circle. Phase I requires the rider to commit to riding in lightness by releasing the rein and relaxing her body. Allowing the horse to carry her passive body is the first step. Learning the nuances of control without the rein is the next step.

The horse will begin to learn to respond to the rider's body as a whole. Where the rider looks repositions her body and directs the horse to follow. Looking to the arc of the circle aligns the rider's body to where she expects the horse to track. Initially, the horse will need the rein and leg aids to follow the rider's movement. Over time, however, he will learn to adjust to shifts in the rider's body alone. For this reason the rider must think of her body as a collective aid and be aware of the messages it sends.

Spiraling in and out on the circle is an important tool. First it gives the rider a measure of control on the circle, because the size of the circle influences the horse's speed. Opening the inside rein leads

During Phase I do not be concerned that because the horse's head is low, he is on his forehand. Many breeds instinctively balance on the forehand. This system will change the horse's natural balance in a thoughtful and compassionate way.

When you encourage the horse to stretch down with *no* weight in the rein, technically he is in self-carriage, albeit not beneath the rider. By relaxing, flexing, and strengthening the horse, the rider helps him shift his balance further back over time without driving the horse into the hand. This approach is distinctive to riding in lightness.

In contrast, the horse will be on the forehand if you ride in the long-and-low position *with* contact in the rein. This, in effect, tilts the horse onto his shoulders. To bring him up into your hand and keep him off his front end then requires you to drive the horse with your leg.

The importance of strengthening the back muscles in order to round the back cannot be overstated. Some horses are so athletic that downward stretching automatically pushes forward impulsion up through the back without encouragement. Most horses will need help to learn how to do this, however. The way to teach this is to first stretch and relax the back. Once you have this access to the back muscles, then you can strengthen the back to hold bend.

Use the horse's ears as an indicator of good position on the circle. If the horse drops his shoulder, the ear on that side will be visibly lower than the other ear.

the horse onto a smaller circle, and he must slow the speed of his gait as the circle gets smaller. He does this by virtue of following his nose, not by the rider retracting the rein. Letting the horse adjust himself teaches balance without compression. By not closing the rein, the horse isn't "held" and must maintain his own balance.

While adjusting the size of the circle, the rider is also teaching the horse to adjust his bend: The inside rein asks the horse to follow his nose, the rider's inside leg and outside rein form the bend, and the rider's outside leg behind the girth helps maintain the horse's hip position.

Enlarge the circle by using the same process in reverse. Opening the outside rein will expand the circle. When giving an opening rein, whether to the inside or the outside, move the other rein to the neck so the horse learns to take direction from both reins. The process of

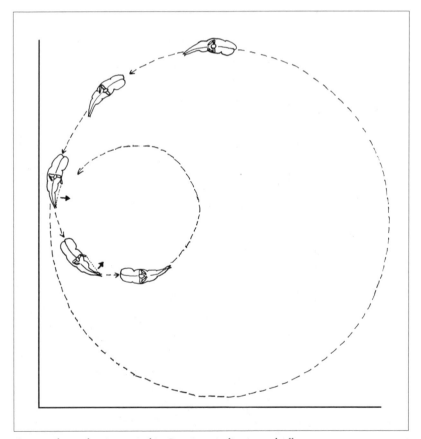

Opening the inside rein to spiral in. Practice spiraling in gradually.

moving both reins also shifts the rider's shoulders to a proper angle in order to direct the movement. Aligning her body to the direction of the horse's movement is important for the rider to understand and experience. Moving the horse between various size circles is also an effective exercise to begin moving his shoulders. In so doing the rider lays a foundation for lateral work under saddle.

Remember, Phase I circles keep the horse on the circle by keeping him correctly on the aids. It is only after the horse develops an understanding of length bend that the rider can begin to give him more independence. While the rider uses her leg to help move the horse forward, it is not a driving leg. As the horse's tension diminishes, the rider should need less leg to feel the same level of forwardness.

THE CANTER IN PHASE I

The dynamic thrust of the canter is not conducive to relaxation or to bringing the head down. Yet, cantering the circle in the Phase I position requires the horse to do both and do it with very little contact in the rein. Some horses, even those responding easily at the walk and trot, will find the Phase I position quite challenging at the canter. Safety also can be an issue: When thrust and freedom cause the horse to lose control, cantering is not advised. This only means the horse may not be ready to canter in the Phase I position until more discipline is acquired, possibly well into Phase II training—this should not be viewed as a problem. Caution is advised, because attempting to canter before the horse is prepared will defeat some of the gymnastic gains already made. The rider can continue advancing the horse at the walk and trot and can develop the circle effectively and even begin lateral exercises with little or no canter work under saddle. Canter on the longe until the horse is willing to relax and canter with the rider mounted. Never sacrifice safety.

Some horses will need continuous suppling to stay light. Others will be light by the nature of who they are. You must feel confidence with the level of relaxation, flexion, and suppleness throughout the horse's body in Phase I before he can come through the bit. Some horses will need extensive suppling each ride no matter how advanced they become. For many of these horses, ending each ride by lengthening and stretching down will bring them out softer the next day.

The rider can unknowingly play a part when the horse loses composure at any gait, but this is especially true at the canter. Longeing with the rider mounted can reveal whether this is a problem. Being longed while mounted can be useful to teach both horse and rider to relax together in a safe environment.

CHAPTER 10

Phase II: Building a Working Frame

Being louder doesn't mean the horse will understand you better. To communicate effectively, relax, be soft, and speak his language.

Phase I prepares the horse to come into a working frame and build strength in Phase II. Gaining access to the horse's back signals when it's time to advance. When the back actively rounds, strength-building can occur. Longitudinal bend over the horse's top line also releases the horse to the rein, positioning him to savor the bit.

When the horse tilts his pelvis back, it brings the haunch under. This serves to lift the chest and lighten the front end. Even though the neck starts off relatively low, the horse is positioned to savor the bit. As the horse shifts weight back, his head and neck will rise proportionately. Bringing these factors together to create a working frame is the goal of Phase II.

Developing the working trot.

SAVORING THE BIT

Savoring the bit is the culmination of lightness. During the process of achieving academic self-carriage, the horse comes to regard the bit in a way that is unique to lightness. He learns to appreciate the bit for its delicate offerings—the freedom to lift the bit, hold it on his tongue with no fear of harm, and allow energy to travel around his mouth and bit with neither obstruction nor undue notice.

BUILDING A WORKING FRAME

As the horse relaxes in Phase I, the rider uses the giving rein to release contact with the bit and send the head and neck down. Now, in Phase II, the soft and/or fixed rein replaces the giving rein in order to maintain the release of the jaw and poll as longitudinal flexion. Flexion increases over time as the horse's balance shifts back until a near-vertical head position and a higher neck carriage is consistent.

The rider makes the transition to the Phase II frame by flexing the inside rein or rotating the wrists up and/or squeezing and releasing the fingers to create a soft give-and-take vibration in the rein. When the horse's jaw relaxes and the poll flexes, however momentarily, the horse begins to savor the bit and ride "through the hand." The horse's intermittent release to the rein is the key step that marks the beginning of Phase II training.

Some horses will give in the jaw and poll quite easily. Others, especially horses being rehabilitated from harsh rein treatment, can have real difficulty with the concept. When the horse is not willing to flex to the soft rein, the fixed rein is used to insist. To fix the rein, the rider shortens the rein length, creating an uncomfortable, solid connection to the bit. The connection is held firmly until the horse releases to the pressure. As the horse flexes to the fixed rein, the rider immediately softens the rein.

By holding the hand firmly on the horse's neck or saddle, the rider can fix the rein securely so that if the horse leans hard into the rein, he can't pull the rider's hand or body forward. With no give whatsoever, the horse must choose between maintaining the uncomfortable position or flexing. Some horses will still resist flexing; nonetheless, given the time to decide, release is the only real option. The lesson of the fixed rein is that the horse should always yield.

All horses need to learn to release to the fixed rein. Teaching the horse to use that release to then bring impulsion forward is more complicated and is the ongoing lesson of Phase II. Nevertheless, teaching how to respond to the fixed rein puts both horse and rider on the path to lightness.

After he releases to the rein, the horse is poised to savor the bit. The rider uses the moment of release to the rein to ride the horse forward. When the horse strides forward with no resistance in the rein, he is in self-balance. Each stride in which the horse is able to balance builds strength. Whenever the horse leans on the rein, the rider must fix the rein and start the process again.

By shortening the rein length, little by little, the rider shifts the horse's point of balance further back. The horse is asked to maintain a degree of the flexion that resulted from his release to the bit. If his head and neck can't revert to the prerelease position, he must either adjust his frame to carry his own balance or lean on the rein. It is this delicate shift-and-balance process, stride by stride, that teaches the horse how to improve his balance and develop an understanding of lightness at the same time.

As the horse learns the lesson of the fixed rein, the rider needs to learn a lesson as well: Although the horse may pull against the fixed rein before he releases, the rider must not pull back. The rider shortens the rein in order to fix a position. It is never accomplished by pulling the rein. Pulling the rein will cause the horse to drop his back, defeating the purpose of the exercise.

The horse learns to find his balance between the point at which he feels the soft connection with the bit and the point at which he feels the solid contact of the fixed rein. This defines his frame. Obtaining a working frame is a gradual progression that must be allowed to happen without force. The horse's willing attitude is vital to achieve a high degree of lightness.

Working between the soft and the fixed rein starts at the halt and continues through walk, trot, and canter. The length of the neck is secondary to the release. The rider should err on the side of a long neck rather than risk compressing the horse's frame and consequently inhibiting his forward impulsion. Impulsion helps to deliver the release by allowing energy to lift the horse's back before he releases. If the rider feels resistance in the rein, it means the horse is not forward. In such a situation, many riders will instinctively drive with the leg. However, speed plays an adversarial role at this time. Instead, the rider should slow the exercise and try again. Relaxation is key in helping the horse find balance and release to the rein. Impulsion can come later once the horse understands how to release to the rein.

Keep in mind that during this exercise only the inside rein is used to flex the horse. Flexing to the inside will connect the outside rein. Both reins then are fixed, defining the frame in which the horse learns to shift his balance. As the horse flexes to release both reins, he engages.

Timing the aids is important for success. Remember, the rider gives the horse options in order to help him make the right choice. If the horse bumps into the rein, let him think about his options. He can lift his head up, drop it down, flex inward, or flex outward. The correct response is to release at C1, which swings the nose back to put slack in the rein. The rider will feel tension in one or both reins until the horse finds the correct release. Maintain the fixed rein until he does. Above all, allow time for the response to become learned behavior.

The release may only last through one stride. The rider's on/off squeezing of the rein should be ready to obtain another release. The horse learns to savor the bit as the rein vibrates. Making the release very subtle allows savoring to begin. Accept any release the horse offers, and repeat the process.

When the horse flexes to the inside rein and then yields, or softens, to the outside rein, he should balance without leaning on either rein. This flexing/softening happens almost simultaneously—the rider feels the horse release to the inside rein, then she squeezes/fixes the outside rein so both reins guide the horse's head and poll. When the horse yields to the contact/connection of the outside rein, it is confirmation that he has shifted some weight toward the hind end.

> Remember the steps that have gotten you this far: 1) relaxing the jaw induces the poll to flex at C1; 2) flexing at C1 then facilitates side-to-side flexibility at C2; and 3) the level of the horse's neck is a function of where he finds balance. Continually flexing to the inside, while connecting the outside rein, enables the horse to find his academic balance through lightness.

Entering Phase II marks the change from relaxing the horse through stretching to relaxing him through flexing. Even though the horse may willingly relax his jaw and send his head down into the Phase I position, he may resist relaxation when asked to flex. By resisting, he avoids engagement and any subsequent shift in balance. There may be days when the horse will readily flex in relaxation and days when he won't. Be aware that his first response may be avoidance.

The process of asking the horse to come into a working frame on the circle is gymnastic in and of itself. The inside hind leg will now carry proportionately more weight and begin to hold it for longer periods of time. This supples and strengthens the back and haunch at the same time. Thus, the more often the horse flexes, the more he strengthens and will be able to maintain more strides in flexion.

Although riding in lightness focuses on relaxation, it does not minimize the need for the horse to be forward. The rider's own relaxation is critical in converting the horse's free forward movement into strong impulsion. The rider needs to move with the horse's motion. Remember that any stiffness will block the horse's forward impulsion.

The horse's degree of balance and collection determines his head carriage. As his weight shifts to his haunch, his head and neck will rise in accordance with his degree of collection. The goal of Phase II is to have the head come to a "near vertical" position. By being "near vertical," the horse can release without going behind the bit. Being overflexed, or behind the bit, represents an imbalance and should be avoided.

As the horse accepts the aids and begins to savor the bit, the rider can relinquish responsibility for the circle to the horse. This will confirm his length bend and his response to the aids. Also at this point the rider can begin to sit the trot. She should begin sitting on the circle or through corners but continue to rise on straight lines within the manège. Because the horse is more engaged on the circle, there is a greater chance that he will stay round over his back and be able to support the sitting rider. When traveling on straight lines, however, the top line is apt to flatten, and a novice horse may lack the development to carry the sitting rider.

> Not all training sessions will be productive. If you are not connecting with the horse on a given day, for whatever reason, it's better to wait and train another day. Take a trail ride and review your previous accomplishments.

When relaxed and moving with the motion, the rider should feel the horse's back push up through her seat. Her seat should absorb energy traveling from back to front. If the rider is tense, she bounces against the motion and compromises the horse's relaxation and forwardness. When engagement comes up through the horse's back, the trot for most horses will become easier to sit. If the rider can't maintain a good position, it may indicate the horse needs more strength to lift her seat.

By Phase II the rider should be relaxed in her body, balanced in her seat, and completely comfortable with lightness in the rein. Some riders have difficulty envisioning just how light the horse can be and still feel engaged. They may lose confidence because, with no weight in the rein, it may feel as if there is nothing out in front of them. In order to overcome this misperception, the rider must let go of the notion that she needs a steering-wheel-like mechanism to control the horse. When she has access to the horse's whole body, through her own whole body, there is no need for a solid connection through the rein.

If the horse has a hard time keeping his shoulders level on the circle, you can address this by doing more counter-shoulders-in work. As little as a few days of training time can have an enormous impact on the horse's understanding.

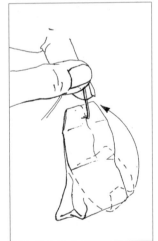

Being a tea drinker, I find the image of a tea bag that has been taken out of the brewed cup provides a useful analogy. When you place the bag on the saucer, the tea settles to the bottom and the bag stays upright. Soon the top of the bag folds over from the weight of the string. When you lift up on the string, you lift the flap without ever feeling the weight of the tea. You can obtain this same weightless feeling when you ride in lightness. The rider doesn't have to feel any resistance from the horse. The horse will respond to the rein lifting on the ring of the bit. Illustrations: Cecily L. Steele

CHAPTER 11

Phase 11: Lateral Work Under Saddle

Ride each horse as if he were the best you have ever ridden. He will respond, and you will become a better rider.

Lateral movement under saddle can begin once the horse consistently releases the jaw and comes through the bit on the circle, even if intermittently. Lateral work is always an integral part of training in lightness, but it becomes the focus of training during Phase II as the horse maintains more reliability on the circle.

Under saddle the lateral exercises are taught in the same order they were taught in hand, beginning with the least difficult—shoulders-in, counter-shoulders-in, then half-pass. Travers and renvers require more strenuous engagement and can be added to the training program to increase the horse's overall flexibility and strength.

This order of training continues the theme of suppling from front to back. The horse achieves a degree of bend while learning the exercises in hand. Now under saddle, the process begins again as horse and rider strive to attain greater flexion. Just as in hand, the rider first accesses the front end to direct the shoulder, then the hind end to direct the haunch. Once she can move the shoulder and the haunch both independently and together under saddle, it can be said she directs all four corners of the horse and, therefore, can direct the whole horse. With access to the legs, head, neck, and barrel, the rider can direct the horse with precision.

The order of teaching each exercise and the importance of allowing time for the horse to develop both mentally and physically cannot be restated often enough. Developing the circle is an important prerequisite before advancing to lateral work under saddle because it creates the relaxation, flexibility, and strength necessary to move laterally and allows the horse time to mature. Work in hand should continue throughout the development of the circle and while the horse learns to ride through the bit. Do not attempt to ride a lateral exercise immediately after it is taught in hand. The horse cannot offer the same results and will resist movement until his body has been suppled into length bend on the circle. The walk offers the best pace in which to teach the lateral aids, but it lacks the impulsion. Trotting promotes forward impulsion and intensifies the elements of movement—stretching, sustaining, and reaching.

Phase II lateral development introduces cadence. Just as each horse has his own natural realm of movement, each horse has a natural rhythm to his gaits. Gymnastic development and an educated response to the aids enhance the gaits by expanding the boundaries of the horse's natural realm. Cadence refers to the embellishment of the natural gait through timing and collection. The transformation of natural rhythm into educated cadence develops during the lateral work in Phase II. To develop cadence the horse needs to engage with equal strength from each hind leg and be equal-strided.

Once the horse achieves good cadence, his degree of relaxation will increase. In turn this greater relaxation elevates overall performance and the response to lightness. This is the circular concept in action: By relaxing into a cadenced stride, the horse releases even more tension from his muscles and joints, which opens more pathways for the smooth forward flow of energy.

Maintaining mental and physical relaxation during each exercise is crucial for achieving maximum development. A comfort zone forms when relaxation is sustained. The rider should continually test the boundaries of this zone, but she shouldn't force the horse to work outside this realm; otherwise the horse may not stay light to the aids.

Lateral exercises teach and test flexion and suppleness from side to side. Remember, the horse must be able to bend laterally before he can round his back. The deep engagement of lateral work strengthens the back and haunch to allow longitudinal bend and flexion, which

Constantly strive for the same degree of flexibility and strength in each hind leg. This allows the horse not only to track in a straight line, but also to track "straight" on the circle. Focus on what the horse needs to improve and the exercise that will enhance his cadence.

positions the horse for advanced academic work through the efficient use of energy.

A brief review of the purposes of lateral work in hand will help the rider understand the expectations of performance under saddle:

- Each movement is designed to target a specific area. For example, as the chest opens to expand the lateral reach of the front leg stride, it also increases its forward range of motion. When the rider has access to move and adjust the shoulders, she also keeps the horse level. Crossing the hind legs articulates the pelvis and teaches the horse to sink the hip. This particular suppling of the muscles and joints expands the range of motion of the hip. Being able to adjust the hips gives the rider more control over the placement of each hind leg. With various degrees of lateral flexion, the hind leg can be placed more toward the horse's midpoint, thereby flexing all the hind-end joints—the hip, stifle, hock, and fetlock. This maximizes strength-building throughout the haunch. As strength increases, so does forward push and the ability to adjust the length of stride.

- The rider's ability to adjust both the shoulders and haunch facilitates correct lateral and longitudinal spinal alignment. This allows for the subsequent change in balance necessary for full and efficient engagement.

- Lateral work is more than just a physical exercise. The horse's thought process matures as well. Through lateral movement, the horse gains an educated understanding of the aids, learning to unify the shoulder and the haunch under the rider's direction. The exercises show the horse how to release through the joints, so he can direct and carry energy laterally. This response to the aids is a learned process—the horse does not instinctively know how to move laterally in an academic sense. The horse gains a new understanding of his own body in the process, and, even when at play, his choice of movement will change. This doesn't mean he will half-pass across the pasture, but the educated horse will balance and move with more sophistication on his own.

Once each lateral exercise is established at the walk, the rider should advance to work at the trot. Establish a good trot on the circle first, maintaining the same rhythm into the lateral direction. This helps the horse push energy up through the back and experience longitudinal bend. Together, lateral and longitudinal bend produce overall suppleness.

While the lateral exercises target specific areas for development, the rider always needs to direct the horse as a whole. Giving the aids only to the shoulders or the haunch causes the horse to drift and avoid the aids. Lateral work increases engagement by teaching the horse to step diagonally. When the horse is equally engaged on each hind leg, he will propel himself forward in a straight line; combined with length bend, he propels himself "straight" on the circle. This deliberate, even stride defines cadence.

Few exercises are done in isolation for their own sake. The rider first stretches the horse by lengthening down in the long-and-low position of Phase I to relax and gain access to the back and sacral area of the loin. That stretching, combined with length bend, develops into longitudinal bend with engagement and collection. Bending supples the horse's body. Together, suppling and stretching align the spine. Once aligned, the long carrying muscles along each side of the spine develop. Lengthening is a prerequisite for stretching. However, lengthening alone does not begin to build strength until combined with the lateral bend.

Some training methods introduce the horse to lateral work through leg yielding. This system begins with shoulders-in because rotations—rather than the straight body position of leg yield—more safely show the horse how to step laterally, reducing the risk that the horse will hit his legs.

Lateral work should play a major role in the horse's daily exercise program. This will increase the degree of agility and strength needed for mature delivery of these exercises as well as other advanced work. Like all training, each exercise is introduced slowly step by step. If the rider asks for too much too soon, the horse will become exhausted, creating soreness, avoidance, and tension.

When training first begins, the horse drifts on and off a straight line because he has no comprehension of what straight is. Don't use the force of your leg to pressure him into straightness. You can slow the drift by applying leg aids, but being against his side all the time will deaden his sensitivity. Although the horse should be generally straight early on, wait until you "direct" the four corners of the horse to be more demanding. First, give him the physical ability to track with straightness. Once this is accomplished, he will go wherever your aids direct him.

The cardinal rule for working laterally, in accordance with my whole system, is to teach and allow but never force. Have patience while the movement matures. Focus on the horse's response to the aids, not the reach or scope of delivery. Initially, the horse may not execute each exercise with the same mobility achieved in hand. Remember to keep each side on par with the other, advancing only as the weaker side improves.

It is important for the rider to find the pace in which each horse can balance. This is initially determined by the horse's natural energy level. The amount of energy and athletic ability establishes when to begin lateral work under saddle and what duration can be expected. The higher the energy level, the sooner lateral work can start and the longer the sessions can run. The energetic horse will be able to maintain enough forward impulsion to carry through the exercise without becoming exhausted.

Most lethargic horses, when conditioned and well ridden, can gain the impulsion needed to carry lateral direction, but these horses need more time to develop strength and forward thrust from their gaits. If the rider has to force impulsion, the horse will lose relaxation and concentration, defeating the value of the exercise.

A word of caution is also warranted in instances when there is too much energy. Don't allow the spirited horse to rush the movement. Rushing tends to place the horse on the forehand, or he may throw himself into the movement, exhibiting a false sense of correctness. It is also important to distinguish a natural abundance of energy from energy caused by anxiety. The horse needs to relax to gain gymnastically from lateral direction. Continuing to work when the horse is nervous or worried produces a forced result and is not conducive to suppling.

SHOULDERS-IN

Shoulders-in is important to all riding disciplines, but it is the cornerstone of dressage. Without good-quality shoulders-in delivery, the horse has no base from which to proceed. The importance of developing the movement correctly cannot be overemphasized.

I recommend using wraps or boots during schooling. All horses will make contact with their legs from time to time, even when normally well balanced. You may not always feel this interference when it happens. By using a light-color wrap, marks of contact will be obvious. This experiment can surprise even an advanced rider on a horse she knows well.

If you ride a high-energy horse, it is easy to overlook your outside leg aid when it isn't needed for impulsion. Remember that riding the circle is more than bending the horse around your inside leg. Teach him to track on the circle from your outside leg as well. This lesson is crucial when it's time to begin lateral exercises. Riding circles on the aids prepares the horse to respond to similar aids for executing lateral exercises.

Work shoulders-in under saddle once the horse is consistently through the bit on the circle at both the walk and trot and is well versed with the exercise in hand, exhibiting fluid movement on and off the rotation.

In this system lightness requires deep engagement. In part this is achieved through a four-track shoulders-in. When delivered with correct length bend, the four-track position increases the flexion in all the joints of the hind leg beyond what can be achieved on three tracks. This optimizes strength-building of the haunch while creating lightness in the front end.

There are proponents for both three-track and four-track positions of shoulder(s)-in. Different schools of thought acknowledge both forms of the movement as long as the delivery is consistent on both reins. Horses should work in three tracks first to increase flexibility before attempting the four-track position.

Yoda demonstrates shoulder-in on three tracks.

On four tracks the greater angle to the wall is obvious.

Initially, the academic rider looks for more lift than drive from lateral work. As the horse's delivery matures, his increased suppleness allows the free flow of forward energy to evolve into ample impulsion. The deep angle of four tracks effectively collects the horse's gait as the exercise matures.

Riding the Exercise

The rider asks the horse to walk a small circle, relaxing his jaw and lowering his head as necessary. The rider brings both hands to the inside, moving the horse's shoulders off the track. Using her inside leg at the girth (and optionally placing the whip further back on the horse's side), the rider asks the horse to step his haunch around his shoulder. As soon as the horse begins to move, the rider brings her hands back to center. If the horse wants to walk forward, the rider vibrates the inside rein to release him to the inside. Creating more bend will start his haunch in rotation. This produces a large turn around his forehand exactly as done in hand. After the initial step inward with the shoulders, both the shoulders and the haunch must move out from the circle as the horse rotates.

Be considerate of the horse's back position. Taking some weight off the seat bones offers the horse relief. Shifting weight to the outside stirrup encourages the horse to push up through his back in the direction of movement.

Prior knowledge of the exercise in hand makes the horse familiar with what is expected. However, some horses may still get confused. A ground assistant can help the rider start the movement, thereby bridging any learning gap between the aids used on the ground and those used under saddle.

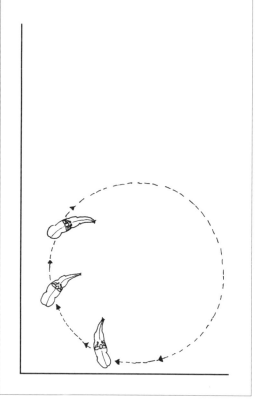

Shoulders-in on the volte. Horses differ in their degree of flexibility, but the rider should strive to align her outside shoulder and the horse's inside hip to the arc of the circle.

Keep the aids consistent but soft. The inside leg touches at the girth and maintains light contact to move with the horse. Shoulders-in needs to be both lateral and forward at the same time. If the horse loses momentum or direction, ride off straight or onto a *volte*.

The initial focus on the rotation is for ease of learning, but do not spend more time rotating than is necessary to create a fluid response. When the rotation flows smoothly, work the exercise down the straight track at the wall. Begin by starting a rotation toward the wall. As the horse's haunch comes to the wall, the rider moves both hands to the outside for one stride and applies her inside leg at the girth for two to four strides of movement in a line. (The rider's hands reposition the horse. Once the horse is on a straight line, the hands move back to center.) Increase the number of strides as the horse maintains relaxation and position. Only use the full manège when the horse can maintain relaxation and impulsion for the distance.

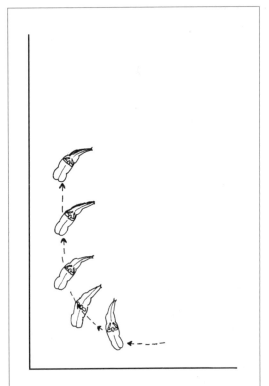

The four-track position requires the horse's shoulders to come farther off the track than required by the three-track position. The horse may try to straighten to make the movement easier. Do not allow the haunch to push outward in an attempt to straighten the bend. Keeping the haunch on the track in length bend is critical for technical correctness. The rider needs to support with her outside leg to maintain the bend. Positioning the horse's haunch closer to the wall can help avoid the hind end evading outward.

Inaugurally, the horse's head and neck should be at or near level with the withers to

Shoulders-in rotation to the long wall. The flexibility of the haunch will dictate the horse's bend. Taking shoulders-in to a curved line teaches the trainer to advance the haunch to a greater degree in order to increase flexibility in the haunch. The exercise requires that the haunch be positioned to take the horse's body straight when it reaches the long wall.

facilitate spinal align-
ment. It is important
that the horse works
the exercise through
his back from the
very beginning. Once
the horse tracks cor-
rectly and fluidly, his
head will rise natu-
rally by virtue of a
stronger engagement.

When the horse is
ready to ride the full
manège, include riding
shoulders-in through at
least some of the cor-
ners. The hind-leg stride
should lengthen to nav-
igate the corner then re-
turn to normal stride so
the haunch is again in
unity with the shoul-
der. This is an impor-
tant aspect of developing engagement.

When teaching shoulders-in, the rider can overbend the horse to activate the haunch. Once the horse's position relaxes and unifies front to back, he can be ridden straighter.

Focus on keeping your seat light. The horse needs freedom to step both in and out of the movement. If he feels too much pressure from your seat bones, it may block his forward/lateral direction. Work to develop your awareness of the position of all four legs as the horse strides—this will teach you how to best sit each individual horse. If the horse needs help stretching his inside leg under, lift off your inside seat bone; if he needs assistance reaching out with his outside leg, lift off your outside seat bone.

COUNTER-SHOULDERS-IN

Counter-shoulders-in carries the same deep four-track angle as shoulders-in. While superficially similar, these two exercises are fundamen-
tally different in what they teach. Shoulders-in unifies the shoulder to
the haunch by concentrating on the movement of the haunch.
Counter-shoulders-in also unifies the shoulder to the haunch but does
so by concentrating on the movement of the shoulder—specifically an
outside turn from the outside shoulder. Remember, this is not an
instinctive way for the horse to turn.

Riding the Exercise

Once again the rotation is used to begin the exercise. The aids are the same as for shoulders-in. The rider creates bend with her inside leg at the girth (the rider's inside leg now faces the wall because this is a counterbend) and supports forward movement with her outside leg behind the girth. If needed, the rider can additionally use her inside rein to help the horse gain bend, allowing the outside rein to follow the bend. Then the rider simply walks the horse around his haunch. This emphasizes the forward lateral movement of the chest and shoulder.

Once the horse can walk freely on the large *volte*, move the exercise to the track. Some riders have difficulty beginning the exercise along the wall. A simple way to obtain the counterbend is by riding diagonally from either six-meter marker to C. At C, begin a counter-shoulders-in circle along the track to the next six-meter marker. At the marker, the horse's shoulders will be on the track. The rider can then

move the horse laterally down the long side by bringing both hands to the outside (of the bend) for one stride. Her inside leg remains at the girth while her outside leg supports behind the girth. The amount of inside rein depends on how much bend the horse will take from the outside rein. Note that the reins come back to the center position once the horse moves forward laterally.

Beginning the counter-shoulders-in at the six-meter marker should not imply that the rider continue for any more than two to four strides. Add more distance only as the horse maintains relaxation and impulsion.

The horse has to be distinctly on the aids for the haunch to moved off the track. The

Counter-shoulders-in on the volte works the horse's haunch in the same way that half-pass does and is therefore a valuable prerequisite for that exercise. As the horse's haunch comes in off the track, his shoulders must cover more ground as he corners around. You may need to slow his haunch to maintain correct movement of his shoulder.

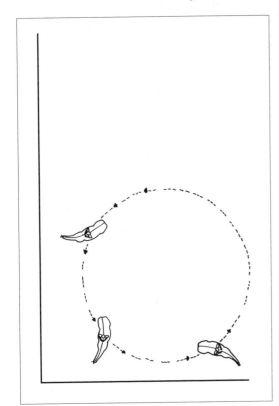

Counter-shoulders-in on the volte. *To produce the most beneficial length bend, the rider strives to align her outside shoulder and the horse's inside hind leg to the arc of the circle.*

rider positions the shoulder, not the haunch. This means the shoulder is on the track and the haunch is positioned away from the wall or fence by virtue of the length bend. With shoulders-in, the horse's position to the wall can help position the haunch correctly while the horse learns to stay on the aids. This strategy can't be employed with counter shoulders-in; therefore, carefully watch the horse's position until the movement is fully understood. Because the horse's face is toward the wall, he can't ride off straight if he loses bend or impulsion (as he can in shoulders-in). Instead, the rider must halt and rotate the haunch around the shoulder to the track before riding off straight (on the same rein but in the opposite direction).

The counter-shoulders-in exercise is not widely used. For competitive school riders it can be an arduous task to drive the horse into the counterbend effectively. When riding in lightness, however, the horse is not looking to the rider's leg to give him impulsion. Consequently, counter-shoulders-in is an extremely effective exercise to open the chest and shoulder to a degree that few exercises accomplish.

Counter-shoulders-in can be more challenging to ride than shoulders-in, but there is no substantive reason to shy away from the exercise as long as caution is taken to maintain technical correctness. Since the movement is not natural, the horse may forget how to move his legs. Then, by having to concentrate on the sequence of his leg movement, the horse can lose impulsion. Developing the movement longer in hand will help the horse retain the exercise and have sufficient muscle capacity to move fluidly. Slowing delivery under saddle also helps to master the movement. As long as

When working counter-shoulders-in in hand, you were cautioned not to close the circle in too tightly because it can compress the hock to twist instead of step. Allow room for each leg to step freely and maintain a forward direction.

Short diagonal to counter-shoulders-in. This will help to achieve the counterbend.

the rider anticipates difficulty and helps the horse through the learning process, the benefits of counter-shoulders-in can be considerable.

HALF-PASS

Half-pass is the first of three lateral exercises that direct the horse forward into the bend. The other two are travers and renvers. All are both mentally and physically challenging. Like counter-shoulders-in, they also require the horse to take all his guidance from the rider.

The strength to hold the half-pass movement is quite demanding. The gymnastic benefit starts as the horse steps the inside shoulder outward into the direction of the bend. The outside hind leg follows diagonally across, sinking the outside hip as the leg steps forward and in front of the inside hind leg. The horse must then lift through the back while the diagonal pair of outside front and inside hind legs step across and into the bend. There must be sufficient strength in the horse's back to balance the entire sequence of the movement.

The academic way to teach half-pass is to simply allow the horse to respond to the aids. Response to the aids is more important than reach of stride. The horse's suppleness and free movement of energy will create scope as the exercise matures.

Riders can make a critical error when they insist that the horse's legs cross. This usually results in overbending the horse and shifts his balance onto the shoulders. When the horse learns half-pass using less impulsion, it is easier for the haunch to balance throughout the exercise, and the joints of the hind legs do not become compressed. This maximizes the gymnastic value of half-pass at this level. The rider can activate the haunch with the outside leg or

Half-pass.

the whip aid to reinforce the lateral direction. In doing so, however, the rider should be careful not to push the haunch ahead of the shoulder.

Riding the Exercise

Begin teaching half-pass from either shoulders-in or counter-shoulders-in. The first method advances the horse to the center line from shoulders-in on a circle. At the center line, the rider weights her inside stirrup as she opens her inside rein. She can motivate the haunch with the whip and apply her outside leg behind the girth. Then opening the outside rein and supporting the bend with the inside rein will move the haunch into the half-pass direction. Take one or two strides in half-pass, then ride off straight or return to shoulders-in.

Opening the outside rein activates the haunch in the direction of half-pass. Closing the outside rein on the neck directs the shoulders into the direction of half-pass. Aids: open rein, touch with leg, touch with whip, close rein to neck.

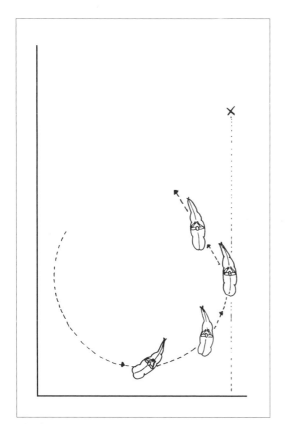

Shoulders-in to half-pass. Ride shoulders-in on the volte. Approaching the center line, arrest the haunches' outward movement (to straighten the length bend). This positions the horse to advance into half-pass.

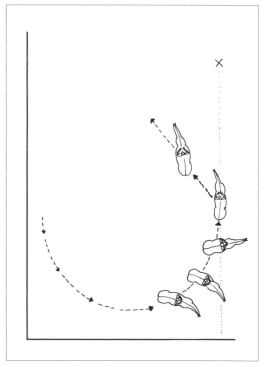

Counter-shoulders-in to half-pass. Ride counter-shoulders-in on the volte. Approaching the center line, the rider advances the horse's shoulder to straighten the bend. Then, as the rider asks for the opposite bend, the horse advances in half-pass. Beginning in counter-shoulders-in emphasizes engagement of the haunch, which helps the horse learn to step into half-pass.

Stiffness in the joints will cause the horse to be tense and lose balance. You can't push him through stiffness. The horse has to move within his comfort zone. Work shoulders-in and counter-shoulders-in to increase suppleness before continuing in half-pass.

The second method starts from a counter-shoulders-in rotation toward the center line. When the rider changes the bend at the center line, the horse is positioned into half-pass as he moves diagonally towards the wall. The haunch is mobilized in either of these positions, enabling it to step into half-pass with enough impulsion to carry several strides correctly.

Begin teaching half-pass from the walk, but move quickly to work at the trot. The impulsion of the trot helps keep the horse's forward momentum in the diagonal direction. The horse may lose relaxation until finding the balance that allows him to move into the bend. To accommodate this, acquire relaxation at the walk, working only short intervals at the trot. Trotting when the horse is tense restricts free forward movement. Do not trot longer than the horse can maintain relaxation. Once the trot stays relaxed, the muscles soften to push the full strength of the impulsion into the bend. This is when the gymnastic benefit of the exercise is realized and overall enhancement of the movement takes place.

Note that both methods of teaching half-pass begin at the center line, not at the wall. The full view of the open manège can overwhelm the horse. The distance across the school can be daunting. Furthermore, the horse most likely lacks the strength or mental discipline to advance the movement very far. Worry in the horse's mind can create a defeated attitude even as the exercise begins. By starting at the center line, the horse will perceive the end of the movement as being at the wall, even though the rider may not even go that far.

Later, the rider should take advantage of the center line in a different way after the horse works fluidly in half the manège. By riding half-pass from the wall to the center line, the horse has visual encouragement to open the reach of stride without tiring over the full distance. Coming to parallel at the center line insists the horse align properly and requires the rider to control the movement with the

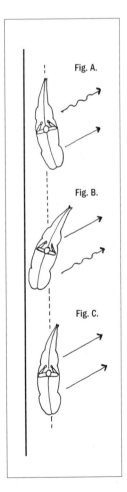

Fig. A.

Fig. B.

Fig. C.

Straight in half-pass. The goal of half-pass is to unify the horse front to hind while maintaining impulsion. Fig. A. If the haunch is allowed to lead, the movement of the shoulder will be uneven. Fig. B. If the shoulder is allowed to lead, the movement of the haunch will be uneven. Fig. C. Unified movement front to back creates free and fluid impulsion.

aids. This enables the horse to learn how to end half-pass without depending on the wall.

Not all horses will be ready to work half-pass this early in the training process. Do not assume every horse fluid in shoulders-in and counter-shoulders-in can go immediately to half-pass. Some horses will need to develop more strength and maturity. The ability to release the joints of the hind legs indicates when to proceed. This is measured by the straightness of the half-pass along a diagonal line. If the line is crooked, the joints in all four legs are not releasing equally. The horse simply isn't ready and won't benefit from half-pass at this time.

Don't regard postponing half-pass as a problem. Carry on with shoulders-in and counter-shoulders-in until the horse gains the ability to work straighter. Pushing half-pass without ample preparation forces the movement and teaches evasion. The horse needs to be able to trust the rider to stay within his current working realm. It is that trust that maintains relaxation and willingness. The rider's job is to prepare and allow.

Once the horse matures in half-pass, the rider should take note of how he responds to the aids. The horse should bend around the rider's inside leg, while taking direction from the outside rein. He should follow the rider's weight in the inside stirrup and move forward into the bend. When the horse will half-pass from the weighted inside stirrup alone, a highly academic level of half-pass has been achieved: The horse moves purely as a function of his bend.

If the horse has a mental block about moving into the bend, you can teach travers first (see below). Some horses learn half-pass more easily as a progression from travers, because moving next to the wall—versus moving across an open arena—is easier to understand.

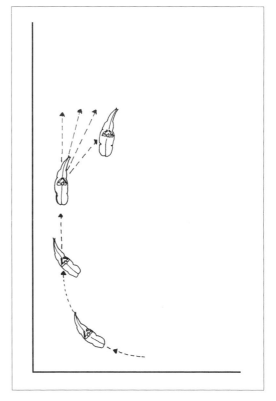

Travers to half-pass. Moving in travers flexes the hip, enabling the horse to move readily into half-pass. The rider looks for movement with evenness of stride. She can adjust the angle of the diagonal line of half-pass to match the horse's level of flexibility. The steeper the line, the more difficult the movement will be.

Some may never pursue this level of sophistication. Nevertheless, it is important for all riders to understand and appreciate the nuances of how advanced and subtle the aids can become. Riding in lightness challenges the rider to teach a movement and then let the horse respond to the minimum aid necessary.

TRAVERS

In this system, travers is the four-track delivery of "half-pass with shoulders to the wall." This is a slightly different interpretation of the more commonly held definition of travers as "head to the wall," a quasi two-track movement. When executed in the progression of half-pass, travers focuses on the placement of the horse's shoulders close to the wall. This increases the gymnastic degree of difficulty on both the shoulders and the haunch because the bend has been increased.

The suppleness and lift achieved through travers is very different from what is developed through shoulders-in. Moving into the bend

This photo of travers captures relaxation into movement. Think of "forward" as acceptance of (any) movement. It is this acceptance with relaxation that allows full and free impulsion without force from the rider.

increases the gymnastic reach of the haunch. The pelvis rotates, allowing the hind legs to stride deeply under the horse.

Riding the Exercise

Start travers from the trot, having first established rhythm on the circle. The aids are the same as half-pass: The rider's inside leg creates bend, then she allows the horse to take the outside rein, opening the outside rein if necessary to send the haunch. Her inside leg remains at the girth, with her outside leg supporting slightly behind the girth.

The horse must move fluidly for travers to have value. The rider should acknowledge the difficultly of the exercise and accept any honest effort from the horse. Initially, limit the exercise to one or two quality strides before moving off straight. The rider increases the number of strides as consistent energetic rhythm can be maintained.

Using travers on the *volte* means circling the horse with the haunches bending in. The rider positions the haunch to the inside of

This and the previous photo show the reach of travers with each stride.

the shoulders on the circle. Do not push the haunch to the inside. Pushing the haunch into position may disconnect the horse's length bend. The haunch would then drag behind the shoulder. The bend must be unified front to back for the movement to flow freely. Travers clarifies the fluidity of engagement by testing the horse to the aids and working the inside hind leg intensely.

In travers the horse's shoulder is close to the wall, which can trigger the shoulder to drop. If the rider fails to recognize the evasion, the horse's weight will shift forward onto the shoulder and into the rein. In lightness, balance is not sustained through the rein. The rider can assist but should only agree to carry the horse momentarily. By allowing the horse to understand moving into the bend in half-pass first, she has the opportunity to work travers in the same fashion (although with more gymnastic bend and angle). This creates a solid understanding of each movement as being independent of each other. To maintain this independence, it is preferable to introduce travers after the horse can half-pass from the wall to the center line in an advanced manner.

All of the lateral exercises require a great deal of impulsion to mature their delivery. Remember, the horse can't fully engage if he isn't relaxed—it is the free flow of energy that creates impulsion. Relaxation, flexion, and strength allow energy to flow forward freely and produce fluid and engaged movement.

A travers-to-halt transition tests the horse's correctness and fluidness. By holding the position while halting, the horse confirms a correct execution. Without complete relaxation the

How to corner: As the horse enters the corner, he loses the guidance of the wall. Advance the shoulders to guide the haunch around. This is the learning process of half-pass— the haunch must move in half-pass while the shoulders advance.

horse is likely to wriggle out of travers during the transition. When correct, the horse should also be able to depart from halt to trot in travers.

RENVERS

Renvers is the most demanding of all the lateral exercises. An examination of the photos that follow illustrates why. The horse moves into the direction of the bend while on four tracks. (Note: Do not ask a young horse to work in travers or renvers on four tracks with deep flexion.) To corner, the haunch must step to the outside of the shoulders. It takes enormous strength and concentration for the horse to maintain balance and rhythm in the renvers exercise.

Like shoulders-in and counter-shoulders-in, travers and renvers are similar movements for the horse when ridden down a straight line. The exercises become distinctly different in corners or on the circle.

A traditional view of travers.

Riding the Exercise

Start renvers from the center line at *X* by moving in half-pass toward the wall at walk. Before reaching the wall, advance the haunch toward the track. Initially, the horse should not be asked to continue the movement past that brief advancement of the haunch. When the horse is willing to engage that more demanding position, the rider can continue the exercise for one or two strides along the wall. Add more strides as the horse strengthens to hold the position. The rider should change the exercise immediately if the bend or forward energy is compromised. If the horse shifts onto the shoulder, change to shoulders-in to regain balance. Be considerate—this movement is complex.

Cornering intensely works the haunch, which must stay in the outward bend all the way around the corner. Progress to a second corner or to a circle very cautiously. The horse must be prepared to sustain the engagement.

Renvers positions the outside hind leg beneath the barrel. The rider can use this highly engaged position strategically. As the exercise moves out of the short side corner, the horse's head is positioned straight down the diagonal line. Asking the horse to then move off straight produces very engaged forward action—ideal for an extension.

Yoda is photographed in each stride of renvers along the wall. If the horse can't fully balance length bend, he will creep away from the wall as he travels down the long side. The rider helps the horse balance through small half-halts in the outside rein. The rider should release the horse to move off straight if he stresses over responding to the half-halt.

SUMMARY OF LATERAL WORK

The deep engagement of work on four tracks essentially develops collection at the walk and trot as the horse learns to move laterally. This level of engagement with lightness to the aids is only obtained through relaxation. Whenever there is tension in the horse's delivery, the rider needs to turn to an easier exercise or the circle. Returning to a comfort zone will regain the lost relaxation. Remember that any rider can force a position on the horse. It is the horse's willingness to release to the rider and move in relaxation that creates lightness to the aids and transforms riding into art.

Using rotations to work the horse laterally can put the horse onto his shoulder, but the advantages of suppling the whole body outweighs this concern when teaching lightness. Rotations are recommended for suppling the horse while warming up or whenever more suppling is needed.

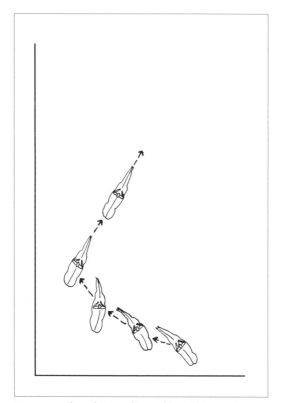

Renvers on the volte *to a diagonal line. This exercise can be used to develop impulsion by flexing the haunch into deep, difficult engagement. As the horse straightens into the diagonal line, the relative ease of movement propels him powerfully forward.*

CHAPTER 12

The Half-Halt

The rider speaks to the horse through her body.

The half-halt creates a momentary pause in action. In doing so it serves two purposes. First, it facilitates the shift of the horse's weight back to balance on the haunch. Second, the half-halt opens a line of communication, giving the horse a "heads-up" to expect another aid (which may well be another half-halt). The perfection of the half-halt is essential for achieving advanced riding.

It takes a great deal of preparation before the horse can half-halt with lightness to the aids. The very concept of lightness explains why: The horse must listen to the rider's seat without looking to the rein for support. Lightness further requires that the impulsion needed to round the back be achieved without the driving force of the rider's leg.

Once the horse's Phase II lateral work becomes fluid, the half-halt can be incorporated into the training program. This means that the horse is able to execute half-halts at the walk and trot first (perhaps even before schooling the canter). Half-halts at canter come later, after the horse is able to balance several consecutive canter strides with lightness to the aids.

By the time the horse achieves a Phase II position at a gait, it is not difficult for him to complete the half-halt at that gait. Delivery of the aids, however, can be challenging for the rider. Effectiveness depends on the rider's subtlety and precise timing. Keep in mind that the bond between horse and rider is the essence of their communication. As much as any learned technique, the ability to develop sensory perception makes the half-halt powerful. In fact, once capable of longitudinal bend, it will be the horse who opens the channel of communication to accept the half-halt aid. This is an empowering event for the horse. After the horse understands, it is up to the rider to create the teamwork that allows the halt-halt to function properly.

The half-halt teaches the rider to use her seat in an advanced manner. As the horse's strength and flexibility improves, the use of the seat as an aid changes. In Phase I the horse interprets the seat as a directional aid. The rider lifts out of the saddle to encourage forward movement or shifts to the inside or outside on the circle to adjust the horse's position. The Phase I seat is not a pressing seat.

As the horse comes through the bit and works laterally in Phase II, the gymnasticizing process focuses on the back. The long carrying muscles along the spine will strengthen, allowing the rider to sit more firmly and brace her back to slow or stop forward movement. The horse learns to pay attention to changes in the rider's seat as Phase II begins, but still, the seat rarely presses against the saddle. As Phase II progresses and the horse is confirmed in longitudinal bend, the rider can press her seat bones down into the saddle without compromising the position of the horse's back. Half-halt training can begin at this point.

The half-halt originates in the rider's center. Her seat bones point straight down, making the firm connection with the saddle that the horse then feels in his back. The energy from the horse's back creates a kinetic connection between the rider's pelvis and her hand. Her hand must support her seat, yet the goal is for the hand to be so soft that it is almost undetectable.

The rider must experience the horse's back pushing up against her seat for the half-halt to be technically correct. Also, for the best results the horse needs be actively forward. If there is weakness in the horse's back or sacral area, it will be more difficult for him to stay round. In such cases the rider will need to sit with finesse. In contrast, a strong-backed horse may need to feel more pressure from the rider's seat in order to respond.

The absence of a solid connection between the horse's back and the rider's seat means the horse has lost the roundness over his top line. By flattening or inverting his back, the horse's forward impulsion collapses; without sufficient thrust the half-halt will disconnect the flow of energy along the horse's spine. Inevitably, the loss of impulsion pushes the horse forward onto his shoulder, essentially negating the purpose of the half-halt, which is to transfer weight to the haunch. Keep in mind that this delicate balancing of power is very difficult for some horses.

Riding the Exercise
The rider initiates the half-halt by pressing her seat bones down while simultaneously flexing her wrist(s) to the inside and upward so the palm(s) face up. Depending on the desired outcome, either one or both reins and one or both seat bones are used. Remember that when the rider steadies her back and seat, she is opposing forward motion. This causes the horse to hesitate, holding his balance under the rider's seat. Then, as the rider releases, the horse's forward motion resumes. This produces the momentary pause in action know as the half-halt. The half-halt connects the rider's hand to the horse's hind leg through the horse's active back.

Although defined as a momentary pause, half-halt is taught by executing a full halt. The rider steadies her back and flexes the rein, holding then releasing in time with the horse's stride. By holding as one hind leg comes forward, then releasing once the hoof is on the ground, the horse will slow each stride until he halts.

Teaching the horse to halt to the seat is an important preparation for riding the half-halt. Walking toward the wall or diagonally into a corner de-emphasizes the rein and emphasizes the rider's seat. By limiting his options, the horse will focus on the rider's seat and not her hand. The horse will slow and stop before or at the wall. Asking the horse to pay attention to the aid maintains his balance while he slows. The horse stops forward motion while keeping his stride complete. When in motion, he will respond to the half-halt in this same way. In time the rider will be able to hold the half-halt aid to produce an immediate halt with the same shift in balance. Naturally, it takes time before the horse understands how to adjust his speed or change his gait

Keep in mind that the aids used to teach become much more subtle once the horse learns. Movement of the hand to deliver an advanced half-halt would be unnecessary.

The walk is an almost diagonal four-beat gait, while the trot is truly diagonal. Deliver the half-halt at walk and trot as the inside hind leg comes forward. Use equal pressure in both seat bones to stop your body's forward movement. To keep the horse round, flex the outside wrist upward while supporting with the inside rein. Let the horse's response determine how pressing your seat needs to be.

while keeping his hind legs engaged. It also takes strength to hold engagement. During training expect the horse to lose balance and fall forward. Continuing the half-halt aid asks the horse to keep trying to balance while not leaning on the rein.

The rider must half-halt with the rein at the correct length in order for the passive flex of her hand to produce shift in the horse's balance. If the rein is too loose, he won't respond, but too short a rein compresses his movement before the half-halt is applied. The correct rein length depends on the horse's release into "near vertical" (see Phase II: Building a Working Frame). By this stage in training, the rider should be skillfully delivering the rein aids and knowing at exactly what length the horse responds. Remember that pulling the rein prompts the horse to pull back, while fixing the rein prompts him to yield.

The horse may need to bump the rein before learning to yield with lightness. Always apply the seat aid before flexing the hand. Closing the hand slowly allows the horse a moment to prepare his response. In time he will respond to the seat aid alone, automatically yielding in lightness. In effect, he will step under to engage the haunch without waiting to feel the rein at all.

Keep in mind that the half-halt is more about balancing than it is about halting, although the two are closely related. The horse learns how to execute an educated halt by learning to balance the shift in weight. Allow the half-halt in motion to develop before practicing immediate halts.

Learning the correct execution of the half-halt is a milestone for both horse and rider. Implementation of the half-halt, however, varies widely. Before becoming proficient with the halt-halt, many riders are still preoccupied with controlling the horse they see out in front of them (i.e., riding the horse's front end). When the half-halt is in place, the rider's focus will inevitably be on the power of the haunch. Once a rider feels the horse come under her seat, lifting and balancing her body, she will be acutely aware that she directs the whole horse by controlling the haunch. The true meaning of riding from back to front then becomes apparent.

At the canter the half-halt is applied as your seat completes its forward roll. Sit and close your outside hand while giving support with your inside hand. Don't worry about which seat bone to emphasize— the thrust of the canter movement will automatically emphasize the outside seat bone. Open your hand and relax your seat to resume the forward motion.

While the intensity of the rider's seat will vary depending on the needs of the horse, the relaxation of her leg is a constant. The rider must be able to use her seat and leg independently. If she supports her seat by gripping with her thighs, it counterproductively forces the horse into her hand. The half-halt teaches the horse to focus on the rider's seat as the most important aid. When the rider's seat stops going forward, it is a signal to the horse to stop going forward, yet keep his stride intact. Therefore, it is the relaxation of the rider's leg which ensures that the horse can rely on her seat for direction.

As stated, the function of the half-halt is to open communication and rebalance the horse. Rebalancing the horse in motion "collects" the gait. The outside rein becomes the "collecting" rein. The rider bends the horse with her inside leg to connect him to the outside rein. The horse will arc with length bend until he feels the connection of the outside rein. From this position the rider sits more deeply and squeezes her fingers (or closes her hand) to deliver a half-halt aid. Collection occurs by changing the flight of the hind leg. When one hind leg stays on the ground for an instant longer, the other hind leg won't extend back as far as it could. Instead of a flatter movement created by a longer stride, the horse pushes upward, producing a shorter, more elevated stride. By continually rebalancing the horse's weight toward the haunch, the shoulders become lighter.

Initially, repeated half-halts may be necessary to keep the horse in balance. But, because the horse's training has taught him to support himself rather than depend on the rein, this is nothing new—the horse already expects to carry himself. Moreover, he already knows how to track the haunch forward freely. Therefore, as the horse becomes stronger, the rider will need fewer and fewer half-halts to collect.

You don't want the horse to bump the rein unless it is necessary. However, to teach the half-halt most horses need to go through a period of bumping the rein in order to understand what you're asking for. Temporarily using a shorter rein to create that bump is fine for teaching the response. Consider fixing your hand on his neck to insure that you don't retract the rein by mistake. Lengthen the rein out longer once the horse learns how to respond. Then gradually shorten again as he gets better at balancing.

CHAPTER 13

Rein-Back

The horse is a reactionary animal with acute protective character-istics. Allow time for him to understand what is expected—or risk confronting these defensive instincts.

Rein-back demonstrates the ultimate utility of the horse's back. Before the exercise is begun under saddle, the horse should be fluid with the delivery in hand: The horse steps back from the haunch, with the back in the raised or coiled position (see Working In Hand). In order to ride the exercise effectively, the horse needs to be supple in his hind-leg joints and be strong enough to carry the coiled position with the rider's weight in the saddle. Suppleness and strength are also necessary to hold the pelvis in the tilted rein-back position. The horse's ability to stay round while transitioning from trot to halt with a rider mounted indicates that he has the necessary suppleness and strength to begin rein-back under saddle.

Mastering rein-back under saddle is a two-step process. The horse first learns the aids to move backward. The second step is to engage himself backward. To understand this fully, think back to the hypothesis of the Phase I position: Lengthening the horse's spine via the lowered position creates the setting for relaxation and the forward flow of energy. Length bend then flexes the horse and engages the haunch in Phase II. As the horse strengthens, his balance gradually shifts toward the haunch until self-carriage beneath the rider is achieved. The natural thrust of the forward gaits facilitates the transfer of balance and allows the rider to be soft with the rein while the horse adjusts. The same principles apply to rein-back, but the horse has no natural thrust for backward movement. In lieu of this, tension in the rein is necessary at first to direct the horse backward.

For the first step, the rider lowers the horse's head and neck into the Phase I training position. As with other exercises, putting the neck level with the withers helps to utilize the back, thereby directing the motion from the haunch and hind legs. In rein-back, however, this lower head and neck position will briefly compromise the expectation for lightness in the rein. During the learning process, there will be some tension in the rein. This doesn't mean that the rider pulls the rein to back the horse. On the contrary, the normal applications of the soft and fixed rein are used. However, if all the tension in the rein is released before the horse learns to follow the rider's upper body aid, the horse has no incentive to step backward.

The process of using length bend to relax, supple, and engage the horse works regardless of whether the aim is forward or backward motion. Once the direction of rein-back is established, the process of

This rein-back shows fluid diagonal leg motion, good longitudinal bend, and softness through the body.

following his bend in reverse strengthens and engages the inside hind leg. The quality and lightness of rein-back develops as engagement strengthens the muscles that propel the horse back. As with all new exercises, while the same muscles may be used, the nuances of the new movement require a different tone and memory. Allow time for this development.

Make no mistake, rein-back is a demanding exercise. Initiate the movement only when the spine is in the correct position. Caution is advised here because repositioning the horse after the backward steps begin is very difficult, and correcting an erroneous response, once it is allowed to develop, can be problematic.

Riding the Exercise

Begin rein-back by halting along the wall. In this case, the rider should not look for a square halt—having one front leg forward facilitates the first step back. After halting the rider lightens her seat bones in the saddle by weighting the balls of her feet. Next, the rider lifts up on the rein on the same side as the forward-most front leg and vibrates it to confirm the release of the horse's jaw. Then, the rider relaxes her waist and shifts back from both shoulders. The act of leaning back will create tension in the shorter rein. As a result, the horse should shift weight to the haunch. The forward front leg should follow the shift in weight and take one step back. The rider can press lightly at the girth (on that same side) if the horse's leg sticks to the ground and does not move. To continue more steps backward, the rider keeps her shoulders back, alternating tension in each rein to move each front leg. As the rider allows tension in one rein, she supports with the other rein to limit overflexion and keep the horse's body straight while he backs.

Do not conclude that using the rein to move the horse's front legs is the same as the horse pushing backward from the shoulder. Rein-back is a two-beat gait—the diagonal front and hind legs move at the same time. Equating the rein aid with the forward front leg becomes an indirect way to move the diagonal hind leg.

The rider should not expect the initial rein-back to be balanced through the haunch. Teaching from the long-and-low position asks the horse to utilize his back as he shifts his weight to the haunch. However, the horse must supple to the backward flow of energy in order for the hip to lower and the head to rise to support the rider in longitudinal bend. If the horse's back inverts, stop the exercise. Losing roundness breaks the flow of energy, causing the horse to compensate by pushing back from the shoulder. If this happens, the rider should walk forward to correct the horse's position before beginning the exercise again.

The preliminary in-hand work should help the horse deliver rein-back with the correct two-beat rhythm. The gymnastic merit of the exercise comes from the flexion of the leg joints. A slow but deliberate pace accommodates an elevated stepping action. Allowing a faster delivery can cause the hoofs to slide backward, drag, or remain low to the ground.

Each exercise teaches the horse to think about ways to release or yield to pressure. Prior to rein-back, the exercises under saddle combined a release with the forward flow of energy. Now the horse

If you feel the horse resisting movement or he locks his legs in place, you can "rock" the horse back and forth without ever requiring him to take a step backward. Simply ask the horse to shift his weight back to his haunch by relaxing your waist and leaning your upper body back. Then bring your body forward again to shift him forward. This simple exercise asks the horse to follow the transfer of your weight.

Yoda is unwilling to back from this position. If, in the training process, the rider presses the horse back from a bad start, the movement will be awkward and rigid and won't teach the right body position. Once the horse learns to balance rein-back correctly, he will be better able to adjust from a bad departure.

must learn to channel energy from his haunch backward. Moving the front end without benefit of forward impulsion requires the horse to think differently about engagement. Inaugurally, he may find it difficult to understand how to lift his shoulder to yield his body backward.

At this level of training, the rider should expect the horse to consistently release the jaw and poll with the first feel of the rein. Normally the rider softens to the release. To begin rein-back, however, the rider does not soften, causing the horse to seek another option. The horse may then release laterally, which is why a supporting rein is needed to maintain straightness in his body. When the rider still doesn't soften, the horse should flex the poll even more, bringing him behind the bit. This extra release signals the rider to lean back with both shoulders. By leaning, she maintains tension in the (one) rein. The horse's weight will follow her back. Initially, this shift may or may not produce a step backward, but it should clearly transfer energy to the haunch. The feet will eventually move. The rider stops the request for rein-back by coming forward with her shoulders, thereby softening the rein.

Being fluid with rein-back in hand helps the horse start the exercise under saddle. Some horses will have difficulty correlating the two exercises because the aids are different when the rider is mounted. The horse must also adjust to the rider's weight on his back. When the horse hesitates or shows confusion about moving his legs, a ground assistant can be helpful to guide him back during the first few training sessions. Be compassionate—the horse· is learning to balance the rider's weight with his back in a highly engaged position. Even strong-backed horses should be sat on lightly and worked slowly. The rider can ask the horse to rein-back several times but should limit each request to one to four steps. Allow the horse to supple and strengthen before backing in segments of more than four strides.

In order to confirm the aids during the first step of rein-back training, it is important to keep the horse straight. The horse may want to swing his haunch off to one side as he steps back. Positioning the horse along the wall, as well as maintaining a supporting rein, will help preserve straightness.

Using the diagonal rein aids of rein-back helps the horse become academic with the rein. It defines each rein as separate and independent from the other. Rein-back teaches the horse to lift each correlating front leg as a response to the rein.

After the horse is confirmed in short, straight segments, adding a controlled bend to rein-back has additional gymnastic benefit. Initially, the rider changes the direction of the haunch by shifting the horse's shoulders. If the rider wants the haunch to bend right, for instance, she moves both hands to the left, taking the horse's shoulder off the track. By moving her hands in this direction, she induces the length bend that will direct the horse's haunch to the right. Engaging the inside hind leg through changes in the length bend shifts his weight back. Over time this engagement builds strength and extends balance. As the horse increasingly balances with the haunch, the shoulders lift, bringing the head and neck up in the process. The resulting lightness in the rein is what allows the rider to direct rein-back solely from her shoulders without help from the rein. Eventually, the horse will respond to changes in her body position alone. (The advanced horse will rein-back when the rider merely draws in her abdomen.)

As with the forward gaits, quality and lightness in rein-back develops with the horse's strength and maturity. Be mindful of the horse's energy level in rein-back. Initially working short routines is ideal. Ask the horse to rein-back, come forward, and then rein-back again. This helps supple the muscles to transfer energy and to hold balance in both directions. These short back and forth segments should be worked both on straight and curved lines.

After the horse fluidly delivers short rein-backs, focus on longer segments. Describing serpentine lines and circles serves to strengthen engagement. Begin rein-back on a twenty-meter circle, traveling only as far as the horse maintains rythm and relaxation. Walk forward when he loses position and begin the exercise again. Change the direction of the circle to strengthen each side on par with the other. Only increase the distance on the circle as the weaker direction strengthens. Once the horse can describe a full twenty-meter circle, the final progression for rein-back is to describe ten-meter figure eights. This sharper length bend makes engagement more strenuous. Once the horse is fluid with the figure eight in rein-back, his forward gaits should be highly engaged as well.

If the horse has any natural crookedness or unevenness of stride, he may veer his haunch off to one side when you rein-back. While this should not be tolerated long term, you can use this predisposition to show him how to follow his body around in rein-back. Allow him to swing to one side in rein-back, then change his bend using serpentine lines to work both directions. Later he will follow your body aids to keep his rein-back straight.

Your body's relaxation is extremely important in enabling the horse's backward flow of energy. Don't allow your seat bones to push down on his back. By relaxing your waist and seat and being soft on his back, you send the horse backward in much the same fashion you send him forward. Once the horse understands how to lift and carry you backward, lightness follows.

The rider can lean further with her shoulders and slide her lower legs back alternately with the horse's stride to maintain impulsion or increase the rate of rein-back. The hand does not play a role in how fast the horse steps back.

YIELDING THE CHEST

The purpose of engagement, whether in the forward gaits or in rein-back, is to rebalance the horse to lighten the front end. The phrase "yielding the chest" describes the ultimate lightening of the shoulder as the old masters envisioned it.

Some horses, through breeding or natural athleticism, will naturally—or through discovery—lift the chest to increase engagement. Other horses can be taught the yield once they have sufficient strength to hold the additional change in balance.

Keep in mind that horses can lighten to the aids and perform well in every aspect of this training program without ever discovering this additional lift and its resulting lightness. Yielding the chest is more-than-normal lightening of the shoulder. The idea of lifting the chest

"Yielding the chest" is not an exercise in itself but a position that can be achieved after the horse is strong and flexible.

higher is a lofty, but attainable, goal that can distinguish the top equine performers.

The rider cannot command the chest to lift without compromising the back nor can she pull the horse's chest higher. The horse must find the yield himself. Rein-back provides the format in which many horses can learn. The power of the back and haunch, as evidenced in exaggerated lowering and tilting of the pelvis in rein-back, stimulates the horse's ability to maximize lift.

Typically, horses with a naturally flat body carriage or those ridden in the lower position over an extended period of time (which is sometimes necessary in order for the rider to access the horse's back) will want to remain balanced forward. By raising the rein, the rider can coax a response from the horse. Yielding the chest requires the horse to "think outside the box"—he has never been given this aid before. But if he obeys and has sufficient strength, his chest should lift as his neck rises with the rein. Only release the rein when the chest lifts higher. Any elevation will be felt under the rider's seat. Though this is only a slight change in overall balance, the result will be a very distinct sense of lightness. The horse's front end will seem to float above the ground.

While rein-back places the horse in the best position to find lift, the practice of using the rein to lift the chest can be applied at any time, in any exercise. Just be aware that the yield upward will come in very small increments. Acknowledge each measure of lift that the horse offers with an immediate release of the rein. This acknowledgment encourages the horse to find more lift (to the degree that his strength allows). For some horses yielding the chest can become a game of who can release faster. This level of communication defines the ultimate bond between horse and rider and brings body language to a truly profound level.

CHAPTER 14

Developing the Canter

*Learn to advance without tiring. When both horse and rider relax,
all their energy benefits the exercise. That is the goal of lightness.*

Roundness and balance are coexistent and inseparable from one another; together they allow the ultimate flow of energy. The horse can have one without the other, but without both he will not obtain the cohesive unity that is the goal of riding in lightness. It is at the canter that this harmony is most obvious even to a novice observer.

The canter only becomes gymnastic once the horse is through the bit and round through the back; even at a modest level, this is engaged collection. Concentrating on the canter before the horse has the strength to hold the rider in this position will not be productive.

To execute the gymnastic canter is far more difficult for the horse than many riders might think. While some amount of collection is present whenever there is release through the bit, cantering in true academic form is advanced work. The horse's ability to come through the bit and collect at the walk and trot does not necessarily mean he is ready to work the canter with the same sophistication.

With respect to the horse, there are always two factors to consider before undertaking any advancement: the condition of his body and the state of his mind. While the order of training seeks to prepare both factors together, the individual nature of each horse makes it more of an art than a science. Developing the canter past the Phase I position is one example where the horse's mental maturity may lag behind his physical capabilities. Even an otherwise calm horse can have difficulty combining the release of the jaw and poll with the forward thrust of the canter movement. If the horse is challenged by the canter under saddle, develop him further on the longe.

Unlike other gaits, the canter isn't significantly improved by continuous cantering. Once the horse releases to the rein at canter, two things will improve the consistency of his strides: By changing gait, upward and downward transitions serve to rebalance the horse's weight back. Half-halts will then rebalance the gait in motion.

This chapter discusses how to obtain the initial release at the canter and then describe the gymnastic routine used to develop collection. When the rider is able to affirm the following points, advancement can begin:

- Cantering on the longe is relaxed and balanced, whether with or without side reins.
- Cantering under saddle in the Phase I position is relaxed with no resistance through the rein.
- The horse flexes at the walk and trot at C1, by giving through the jaw, and at C2, by looking in the direction of the rein at the walk and trot.
- The horse keeps his shoulders level on the circle or will correct his position under the rider's direction.
- The horse comes through the bit at the walk and trot. (His willingness to flex and stay light is more important than maintaining balance for long stretches.)
- The horse can remain through the bit while increasing/decreasing the size of circles at the walk and trot or change rein without losing balance.
- The horse is progressing in shoulders-in and counter-shoulders-in at the trot.
- Working in half-pass is a plus but not essential.
- There is reasonable strength and flexibility through the horse's back.
- The horse demonstrates his understanding the rider's leg aids by bending around the rider's inside leg and by understanding that either of the rider's legs can become a "wall" to stop him from falling in or leaning out on the circle.

CANTERING THE CIRCLE

The horse initiates the canter from the outside hind leg. Therefore, the rider's outside aids request the transition. She rotates her waist slightly toward the horse's outside hip. This moves her outside shoulder, hand, seat bone, and leg back in unison. (If she needs the support of the whip, it is held with the outside hand to touch behind her leg.) Meanwhile, her inside leg remains at the girth in order to maintain the horse's length bend.

Begin on at least a twenty-meter circle. Prepare for the canter by relaxing the horse into an active trot. Working at one end of the manège, request the canter after the horse crosses the center line at *X* and advances toward the track so the three solid walls (or fence) will define the circle before the horse again crosses open space. Apply the aids as the horse's outside shoulder comes back. This is when the outside hind leg comes forward to begin the first beat of the canter.

Wait for the horse to relax into a good trot, so he can make the transition to canter without resistance in the rein. Forward impulsion

Beginning frame for Phase II canter.

should create the initial "give" to the rein, allowing the rider to be soft with her hands. The thrust of the haunch lengthens the horse's body as he strides forward, and this stretch connects him to the rein. Since the horse knows to release to pressure, his jaw will relax and his poll will flex as he pushes into tension in the rein. Remember, flexion in his poll changes his spinal alignment. Now, energy coming forward from his haunch is directed upward through his back. As the haunch continues to thrust forward, the back rises, lifting the spine into longitudinal bend. However fleetingly, the horse engages and collects with lightness. This is the gymnastic canter.

Experiencing even a brief moment of this form of canter is a powerful feeling for both horse and rider, but don't expect the horse to maintain this level of balance right away. Many riders will be tempted to hold the position with the rein or pull the horse back "into balance," if only in an attempt to show him the way. This is an error: In essence, any force through the rein constitutes riding the horse's front end. The horse must be allowed to release into longitudinal flexion as opposed to being held or pulled, which will only compress him into a frame. Be satisfied with whatever lightness the horse can offer, even if that means only one or two strides. Any release opens the door to collection.

Some horses will find it extremely difficult to relax and release at the canter. If the initial upward thrust into the canter does not produce a release to the rein, the rider should return to trot and compose the horse by using the Phase I position. Once he is relaxed, the rider can use the soft rein to caress him into a willing release.

Increasing the bend may also encourage the horse to release. The rider can temporarily request more length bend with her inside leg as she uses her outside aids to initiate the canter. This causes the horse's ribs to arc outward, prompting his whole body to release to the inside of the circle. This additional length bend will induce the horse to release through both reins, provided that the rider is sufficiently relaxed. When using this tactic, the rider loosens her outside leg to encourage the outward articulation of the spine and rib cage, which will help keep the horse soft and relaxed in his forward movement. Even slight repositioning of the spine promotes relaxation and free

You always want your body to help the horse move in the intended way. Just as sitting lightly makes it easier for him to push energy up through your seat, relaxing your outside leg as he bends around your inside leg gives the ribs room to arc outward, filling the void. Remember, a relaxed position is still supportive—it's just not pressing or blocking.

forward movement. The rider needs to be careful that in her effort to create more bend she does not retract the rein. If the rein is closed at the canter before the poll flexes, it will obstruct forward impulsion.

Any one of these progressions should produce a few consecutive strides of canter without resistance in the rein. Although the horse is not yet collected, he is learning how to balance the collected position. Whenever there is weight in the rein, however, the horse's balance has relapsed and he has fallen forward. In these early stages of learning, if you feel pressure in the rein, soften the rein and lengthen down into a rising trot. Reestablish rhythm in the trot before transitioning back to canter to start the process again.

The goal of teaching the canter in this way is to help the horse achieve more and more strides of lightness before losing balance. The rider provides that help initially by transitioning to trot and starting the canter again whenever the horse loses his balance. Once he can maintain several strides together, the half-halt can be used to rebalance the gait as the canter continues. Starting collection through brief segments of high-quality canter shows the horse how to be round and use his body properly from the onset.

DEVELOPING COLLECTION

There are three components to collection: balance, cadence, and impulsion. Evenness of stride, balance and impulsion determine the quality of the cadence. The following discussion explains how to develop the canter into a collected movement with roundness and lightness to the aids.

The outside rein is the collecting rein. The half-halt is the aid used to connect the horse to the outside rein. Momentarily after pausing the horse's forward movement with her seat, the rider then squeezes the outside rein to obtain a release. If the rider also supports with the inside rein, the horse will release to both reins and come into a collected position. The horse needs to be able to sustain good balance, cadence, and impulsion, however, before the rider can fully connect him to the outside rein in self-carriage. A few strides of good canter is the ideal way to build collection.

Some horses will need help understanding the role of the inside hind leg in lifting the back. If the inside hind leg doesn't track well underneath his body, he possibly won't be able to achieve longitudinal bend. If his stride feels uneven, he may be avoiding engagement by not flexing his inside hind leg or not following the curve of the circle. By closing your fingers on your inside rein while turning your palm up, the horse should yield his ribs to the outside and better engage his inside hind leg. This movement of the rein is very subtle. Keep your hand on or close to his neck. Just show him the way to come under and engage as his jaw releases.

The sum of all the prior gymnastic development gives collection its artful quality. A significant level of maturity and skill is necessary to produce collection with lightness to the aids. Before connecting the horse to the outside rein, be sure he is:

- Willing to relax the jaw
- Flexible at C1 and C2
- Understanding of the aids
- Supple throughout his body
- Able to lift his back
- Capable of deep engagement

Once the horse offers the initial release to the outside rein at the canter, the rider helps him maintain balance by moving in unison with his stride. He has no incentive to lift into longitudinal bend if she blocks his free and forward movement. Harshness with the hand or stiffness within her body also inhibits the horse from staying round and being forward. Asking for the canter when the rider is stiff sends the horse stop and go messages at the same time. An educated horse just won't respond, and one in training will be profoundly confused. As the horse becomes more advanced, so must the rider. She needs to address any impediment to attaining unison with his movement.

Once the horse can maintain roundness for three or four canter strides, the half-halt can be used to extend the number of balanced strides. Applying a slight half-halt with each, or almost every, stride helps the horse keep his balance back while continuing to canter. The half-halt is executed on the second beat of the canter, as the horse's inside hind leg comes forward. Timing the half-halt correctly is critical: The rider steadies her seat and closes her fingers on the outside rein as the horse finishes his forward motion. As the horse's motion relaxes her seat back into the saddle, she loosens her hand on the rein. This will keep the horse's inside hind leg on the ground momentarily longer. Slowing the tempo of the stride flexes the hind legs more deeply, thereby shifting weight to the haunch. As the haunch sinks the horse's shoulders rise. As a result, the horse canters with collection and demonstrates balance, cadence, and impulsion.

Most riders function satisfactorily at the walk and rising trot despite a poor seat, but the canter is not so forgiving. If the horse won't come round at the canter, scrutinize his physical condition for any signs of a problem. At the same time cast a critical eye on your riding. By definition, the horse cannot be light to the aids if your hand or body blocks his forward movement. If, in order to keep your own balance, you pull the rein, bounce, or grip, you'll need to compensate by using more leg to drive him forward. When you block and drive at the same time, you invite the horse to drop his back and/or deviate out through his hocks. The horse cannot be faulted for protecting his spine from concussion. In many cases the rider's position must improve before the horse will come through the bit at the canter.

Using half-halts will help the horse stay balanced, but he will still shift forward. Transition down to trot whenever the half-halt doesn't immediately rebalance the horse in lightness. But don't always wait for the horse to falter. Introducing the half-halt into the collection process doesn't replace a vigorous transition routine; rather, the half-halt enhances the progression of collection.

Remain on the circle while teaching the horse how to collect. Length bend directs the inside hind leg into a position of greater engagement. This makes developing collection easier. Then, as balancing with roundness and lightness becomes less effort, ask the horse to straighten his body for short stretches. Start strides of straight movement along the short side of the school or ride two to four strides down the long side before returning to the circle. Adding strides of straight movement teaches the horse how to adjust his balance to his body position. Quickly returning to the circle will help him maintain balance.

Remember that the circle also represents a comfort zone for both horse and rider to relax in what they know. The rider is advised to frequently return to the circle while she is expanding the horse's knowledge and his physical strength. As the rider comes out of the corner, she straightens the horse by sitting straight forward. She will again align herself to acquire bend upon returning to the circle. Gradually increase the straight segments of collected canter until the horse can utilize the full manège.

Don't be alarmed if the canter reveals new resistances within the horse's body. The horse may be elegant at the walk and trot but dramatically unrefined at the canter. This rigidity occurs because muscles perform differently when the gait changes. The effect may be felt in one or both reins. The horse is not being bad—he is just showing what he can and can't do. This signals the rider to help him let go of the lingering vestiges of stiffness and tension that remain in his body. Accept this as part of canter training. Once this tension is released at the canter, the horse's increased suppleness and fluidity will benefit all other movements. Working shoulders-in and rein-back between canter segments can help to keep the horse supple and further relax the canter.

To collect the canter, use mini half-halts. By closing and opening your fingers on every stride, the horse rebalances with each step. Start with just a few strides of collection before transitioning down or continuing the canter in a longer frame. Don't overtax the horse by asking for too much too soon.

Working the canter also calls attention to the horse's level of conditioning. While working at the trot can seem effortless, he may tire easily at the canter, especially if tension exists. Avoid cantering the horse out of breath; he can't absorb the lesson when he is physically stressed.

The horse will develop cadence at the canter once he is in academic self-carriage. Keep in mind that enhancing the canter, or any other gait, through gymnastic development shouldn't take the horse out of his natural realm of movement. Never insist on a level of collection that the horse cannot maintain. If there is weakness in any of the building blocks, his collection won't be ideal. It is the rider's responsibility to figure out whether the horse is working at capacity or if more suppleness, strength, and/or relaxation will improve his collection. Be respectful of his natural gaits.

CHAPTER 15

Transitions

Allow the horse to make mistakes. Then help him understand a better way.

Transitions are made in some fashion from the very first stride of training. This chapter discusses how to approach the changing of gaits as the horse advances through his training. Understanding the dynamics of the gymnastic exercises in each training phase helps the rider appreciate that academic transitions emerge out of the horse's overall relaxation, flexibility, strength, and comprehension of balance.

The horse will not be able to correctly balance a transition under the rider's seat until he can carry forward motion with longitudinal flexion. Therefore, pending the execution of the half-halt, the rider should allow the horse to lengthen his frame into each transition. This same process applies to all changes of gait, either up or down. Transitioning from canter to halt is conceptually the same as departing from walk to trot. In each case, the educated horse is asked to shift weight back to balance and initiate action from the haunch. This is a learned process.

Most saddle horses are inclined to shift forward to change their gait. Lifting the head and inverting the back places weight on the shoulder. As training disposes the horse to incrementally shift his weight to the haunch, the rider's challenge is to recognize his current point of balance and ride transitions commensurate to that level of training.

As the rider focuses on relaxation and forward mobility in Phase I, the horse is allowed to remain within his natural realm of balance.

Upward transitions encourage the horse forward in the long-and-low position. Inward spirals help the horse to slow or stop forward movement. There is little contact with the rein.

In Phase II, as flexibility and strength increase, the haunch will begin to play a greater role in balancing transitions. As the horse comes through the bit, his frame gradually shortens. There is a direct relationship between the length of the horse's frame and the length of the rein. The rider continually shortens the rein as the horse's frame shortens. The horse is allowed to lengthen slightly as both upward and downward transitions are made. (If the rein shortens too quickly, the horse will be pulled into a frame. When the horse is pulled, he is less likely to balance through the transition; instead he will turn to the rein for support.)

By not compressing the horse with the rein, the freedom of forward movement taught in Phase I can be combined with the length bend taught in Phase II. This produces the flow of energy that, in part, induces the horse to round his top line. Once the rider feels this lift under her seat, she begins teaching the half-halt. (This is normally midway through Phase II.) Transitions become a function of the half-halt once the horse becomes aware of how to lift and hold the rider. Transitions will become engaged at the walk and trot first. Until the horse comes through the bit at canter, continue to lengthen up to and down from the gait.

Balanced transitions require composure as well as strength. Practice some engaged transitions, then allow the horse to lengthen into others. Don't expect the horse to hold the longitudinal bend and flexion necessary for an academic transition when he is tired. Remember, it is rare for the horse to be purposefully disobedient—be cautious to avoid fatigue and psychological stress.

While upward and downward transitions are similar in concept, the variable factor is impulsion. To make an upward gait change, the rider moves the horse forward with her seat before applying the half-halt. For downward transitions the rider braces her seat before applying the half-halt. Because the rider can more easily direct impulsion to move the horse forward, it is best to teach upward transitions first.

Remember, the horse must tilt his pelvis for the haunch to come under and arc his back up. If you pull the rein during the transition, you stop the pelvis, making it harder for the horse to lift or hold a round position. Losing bend, or "losing the back," gives you the feeling that you need to drive into the transition with your leg. Be patient. Once the horse balances within the half-halt, his strength will allow his back to rise and hold you during the transition.

Transitions using the half-halt are about your seat, not the rein. You support with the rein without pulling. When the horse is confident that you won't pull, he will relax into the half-halt and be less inclined to invert his back.

Combining the impulsion to move forward with longitudinal flexion at the poll facilitates shifting the horse's weight onto his haunch. It is more difficult for the horse to understand how to make the same shift when slowing or stopping his movement. The greater the speed, the harder it is for the horse to hold his balance back. He will fall forward until the haunch is positioned to keep the balance. Balancing a change in gait requires a good deal of strength in addition to concentration from both horse and rider. Practicing transitions midway through the ride allows the horse time to supple yet stay fresh in mind and body. The following guide suggests appropriate combinations of transitions—and the order in which to teach them—to maximize benefit within each ride:

Think about where you execute transitions. Choose a spot that will encourage the horse to shift his weight back, then use that spot until he associates the aids to what is expected. Transition down when going into the corner. Transition up when coming out of the corner.

Phase II

Halt to walk
Walk to trot / Trot to walk
Trot to canter / Canter to trot
Walk to canter / Canter to walk
Halt to trot / Trot to halt

Phase III

Halt to canter / Canter to halt
Rein-back to walk / Walk to rein-back
Rein-back to trot / Trot to rein-back
Rein-back to canter / Canter to rein-back

Expect the horse to bump into the rein when learning to transition the gait. This bump produces the necessary shift in weight that allows the horse to find his balance within the length of the rein. The horse will begin to adjust his balance before feeling the connection of the rein once he responds to the rider's seat aids, which either encourages or discourages forward movement. When the rider executes the half-halt correctly the horse will, over time, transition without tension in the rein. The length of this learning curve depends on the horse's strength and ability to stay focused through the transition.

CHAPTER 16

Phase III: Counter-Canter

Art is revealed when the difficult appears effortless.

Counter-canter is an important building block in the horse's over-all development. Like counter-shoulders-in, counter-canter works the horse in "counter," or outside, bend. The exercise flexes and strengthens the inside hock and hip, which now refers to the leg closest to the wall.

Gymnastically, the outside bend flexes the inside hock and hip to a degree that is not accomplished through an inside lead canter. Academically, the exercise solidifies the horse to the canter aids while preparing him for flying changes.

As a pure gymnastic workout, the horse can benefit from counter-canter as soon as a canter departure from the trot stays balanced through the bridle. However, until the horse identifies both lead aids with consistency, he will lack the academic discipline to depart into and remain on the correct lead.

To solidify the horse to each distinct lead aid, move away from the outside track of the manège. Practice canter departures from the center or quarter lines. This lessens the horse's predisposition to assume the inside lead. Begin to teach counter-canter after transitions to each lead are fixed to the aids, regardless of location. From that point the exercise is simply a function of riding the horse to the aids. This underscores the old masters' belief that counter-canter isn't taught, it merely asks the horse to respond.

Counter-canter should begin on straight lines. This allows both horse and rider to practice cantering with less length bend than is called for on a normal circle. It allows the rider to verify the horse's ability to track the haunch straight on each lead. The lightness and cadence of the straighter canter position should be comparable to the horse's normal gait in an inside-lead canter on the circle.

How the horse learns to balance in the counter-canter is very interesting. Let's look more closely at the process. Developing the counter-canter on the curved line starts with the horse's body posture being relatively straight. This straightness commits the horse to swing the haunch to the inside, or "lead" side with each stride. This swing is necessary to stretch the reach of the inside hock as the inside leg lands. Then, as the outside hind leg follows in stride, the inside hock flexes downward. At first this hock motion will be stiff, making the horse difficult to maneuver. As the horse supples and strengthens, the inside hock flexes more easily, allowing the counter-length bend to develop. With length bend the inside hind leg will engage closer to the curved line, lessening the exaggeration caused by stiffness. Moreover, as the horse relaxes to the counter-bend, his energy will flow smoothly forward. On the circle, the gentle outward arc positions the inside hock to obtain deeper flexion. The added push that results from this flexion lifts the back and increases muscle development on each side the spine. The deep engagement of the counter-canter also continues to supple and strengthen the haunch. This is the gymnastic significance of counter-canter.

Giving the horse ample visual space is important to the exercise. Corners will be intimidating until the horse comfortably balances

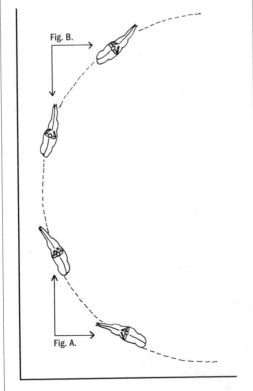

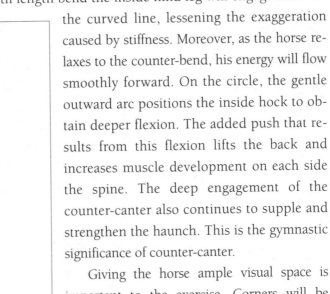

Counter-canter. Fig. A shows the horse avoiding engagement by straightening his body to be able to move the haunch inside the arc of the circle. Fig. B. In order for the horse to flex and accept the counter-bend, he must swing the haunch outward each stride.

Fig. B.

Fig. A.

the counter-bend. Departing down the quarter line or on a long diagonal gives the horse a clear sight line. Transition to trot well before entering the corner to help the horse avoid worry and to maintain his relaxation.

Specific use of the quarter line is advised because the long wall can be as intimidating to the horse as the corner. This is because tracking in the counter-bend changes the horse's perception of his proximity to the wall or fence. In normal bend the horse looks into open space. With even a "straight" counter-bend, the horse looks toward the wall. This makes the wall seem closer, and any actual crookedness in the horse's stride can draw the haunch toward the wall. Fear of colliding with the wall may make the horse want to push away. If the rider applies stronger aids to move the horse straighter or nearer the wall, she forces a more difficult degree of engagement. All horses that don't track properly need time to supple and strengthen in order to straighten, but they first need to be confirmed to the canter aids. Riding counter-canter off the track accommodates these concerns in a nonthreatening manner.

Failure to track with length bend is usually the result of stiffness in the hock or hip. The horse takes an easier path to avoid flexing joints in the hind legs. Suppling and strengthening through shoulders-in at trot will help the horse to flex and allow him to develop length bend.

The ideal vision of counter-canter is that the horse will have no concern whether the bend is inside or outside, only compliance to the lead. However, navigating a circle in counter-bend can send confusing signals to the rider. She must remember that the horse's haunch needs to track to the outside of the shoulder on a curved line. Concentrating on the horse's length bend, relative to the track of the circle, helps the rider apply the aids and sit correctly. The corner or circle should simply happen as a matter of course. Focusing on the shape of the circle alone changes the rider's perception of where the horse will track and can cause her to push the horse around the circle from his shoulder.

It is also easy to think that overbending the horse will help hold the counter-lead. Quite often the rider causes the horse's crookedness by being aggressive. The rider should be attentive with the aids, but remain relaxed and soft to allow the horse to find the correct position of counter-canter within the parameters of the aids. Recognizing that the deep flexion of the hock allows the horse to more easily balance counter-canter with less bend should help the rider teach the exercise correctly.

Riding the Exercise

Starting counter-canter on straight lines permits the horse to adjust his position in small increments and balance straightness on his own terms. Then, adding gentle curves before transitioning down to trot begins counter-canter in earnest. The rider proceeds further along the curve as long as the horse stays composed. Just as the horse had to

The counter-canter demonstrates how the rider can use the wall as an extra aid. At the same time, note that the rider needs to maintain the aids throughout this exercise even if the horse may not appear to need guidance. This is because the rider's habits become the horse's habits. Clear and consistent aids serve to lead and focus the horse. If the rider teaches the aids but also allows the same movement without the aids, she sends mixed messages to the horse, making it difficult to ever "fix" him to the correct aids.

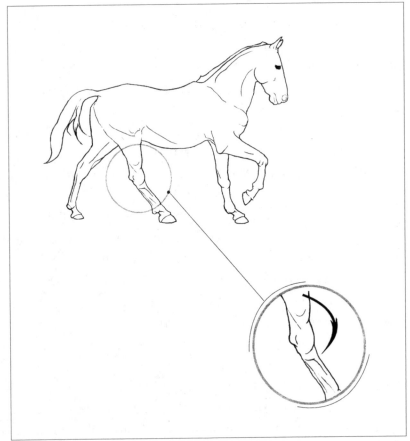

As the hock gains the ability to flex more deeply, the inside (lead) hind leg will engage to the line of the circle. This allows the horse to relax into the outside bend, eliminating the need to exaggerate the outward "swing" of the haunch. The counter-canter then becomes smooth. Illustration: Cecily L. Steele

learn to balance straightness, the counter-bend requires him to rethink his balance once again. This is truly an educational process, and his gait will feel awkward while he adjusts to the counter-bend. Remember that the horse must first swing his haunch into the bend in order to move along the curved line. This exaggerated movement will feel awkward to the rider. To insure that the horse will not feel crowded against the wall or corner, the rider must provide enough space for the haunch. Sitting lightly also encourages free movement of the haunch. The horse normally feels the rider's outside seat bone at the canter; be sympathetic of his need for freedom to now move outward under that seat bone. The haunch will swing further with less resistance on the back.

Yoda in counter-canter.

Suggested exercises for developing counter-canter (beginning with the least difficult):

- In counter-canter ride straight down the quarter line or do long diagonals, transitioning down before the corner.
- Ride a curved line, then transition down.
- Ride through one corner and transition down.
- Ride large-loop serpentines, utilizing both the inside lead with natural bend and the outside lead with counter-bend.
- Ride the two short corners (stay in a confined area so not to fatigue the horse).
- Ride the two short corners and turn down the diagonal line before transitioning down to trot.
- The final progression takes the horse onto the circle or to the full manège. The strength or weakness of each individual horse determines whether circling or riding the full school comes first. Circling develops the entire haunch by targeting the inside hind

leg on each stride. This may be too demanding, however, if any crookedness remains in the horse's gait. Working the full manège allows the rider to straighten the horse along the wall to equalize flexion in both hind legs. Once the horse can navigate through the corners with ease, working on the full circle will be less taxing.

Expect the horse to swap leads during the awkward stage of learning to bend and balance. The lead change may be caused by a loss of balance, or the horse may still try to assume the inside lead. The horse may change the lead on just one leg (either front or hind) or change both in front and behind. This is not bad behavior and shouldn't be reprimanded. Quietly transition down to trot whenever the horse changes lead and begin again.

Asking for rein-back between segments of counter-canter can help develop the counter-lead. Rein-back lightens the horse on the shoulder by rebalancing his weight farther back. By making the haunch stronger, counter-canter also improves the balance and cadence of the canter in general.

A true understanding of lightness recognizes that the bend for counter-canter is manifested from the relaxation within the horse's mind. Teaching counter-canter in lightness gives the horse freedom to discover his balance in the movement without being carried by the rein or forced in any way. The rider cannot impose compliance on the horse. Requiring the horse to submit to any exercise without full relaxation disturbs the learning process.

Some horses will start counter-canter unable to work straight. This may be caused by horse's inability to flex the hock, stifle, or hip. However, the unevenness of your aids can also be a factor. Once the horse will remain in counter-canter, bring him closer to the wall to encourage a straighter engagement. Stay soft with your aids, allowing the wall to position the horse straighter.

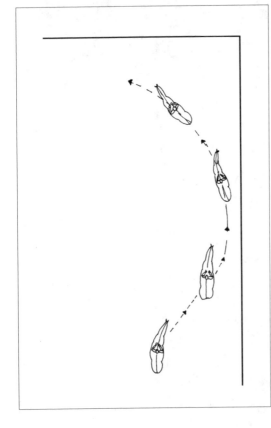

Half-pass to counter-canter. Trot half-pass is an ideal spring-board into counter-canter. Half-pass on the diagonal line and depart into counter-canter as the horse approaches the wall. The horse will be moving in the correct bend to assume the counter-lead.

CHAPTER 17

Phase III: Flying Changes

The horse is a creature of natural instincts as well as learned behavior. The training process asks him to rely on his learned behavior and respond to the rider's aids. Yet, all horses will react by instinct when overstressed. The educated rider knows her horse's pressure point and doesn't push him over the line.

A flying change is nothing more than a canter departure. When put in that context, much of the mystique behind the exercise dissolves. To remain within the scope of this book, the discussion of flying changes is limited to the execution of a single change.

Rather than a gymnastic exercise in itself, a flying change is proof of preparation. Three factors indicate when the lead change can be introduced:

- The horse can canter depart from walk in collection;
- The horse is fixed to the aids in counter-canter;
- Downward transitions are directed by the rider's back and seat and not the rein.

While these prerequisites designate a level of academic achievement, certain physical attainment is also implied. A flying lead change is as dependent on the flexibility of the horse's hind end as on his compliance to the aids. The horse's capability to travel with equal impulsion on each lead is a measure of his suppleness. The rider will feel in her seat when unevenness exists. Do not attempt lead changes until each lead has the same rhythmic beat.

The horse learns flying changes by transitioning from canter to trot and back to canter on the opposite rein. This is called a simple change of lead. A flying change is a function of executing the simple change transitions closer and closer together until the succession eliminates the trot completely. The horse must execute simple transitions fluently before attempting flying changes.

Engagement is crucial for the technical correctness of a lead change. The horse will not balance the change, with no resistance in the rein, without having sufficient engagement. What constitutes engagement will differ between horses. Some horses will be more relaxed in a faster canter. Others will want more collection. Because relaxation maintains the cadence and lift throughout the lead change, the horse's overall degree of composure determines the transition sequence. In other words, there is no standard of engagement for teaching a flying change. Train at the level of impulsion that will make the lead change easiest for the individual horse.

Precise timing of the rider's aids is critical. The canter stride has three beats: Assuming an inside lead, the first beat is made with the outside hind leg. The second beat pairs the inside hind leg with the diagonal front leg. Then, the inside front lead leg lands to make the third beat. There is a moment of suspension following the third beat. The horse initiates a lead change from the outside hind leg. This means that the rider changes her aids on the third beat of the canter so the horse changes lead while suspended in stride. (The precise moment to apply the aids will vary; each horse and rider team will find their own unique timing.)

Riding the Exercise

Begin working simple lead changes from a twenty-meter figure eight. The rider executes the change at *X*. To change direction with the change of lead helps the horse relate to the distinct aids for each lead canter. The rider should first obtain a good relaxed canter. Then, as the horse approaches *X*, straighten the length bend and transition to trot. When the horse breaks to trot, apply the aids for the canter in the

Riding the flying change is very much an art. You can exaggerate the bend of the haunch until the horse learns to execute the flying change to the aids, but don't continue to ride that way longer than necessary. While straightness isn't the most important factor for a single change, it is vital for multiple changes. When the horse's haunch swings, he can't get back into position fast enough to balance another change. Teaching the single change with the same degree of straightness is the goal.

new direction. To do this, the rider slides her outside shoulder back from her waist, shifting her outside hip, leg, and hand in unison.

While this scenario references *X* as the point of lead change, it is only important to make the downward transition to trot approaching X. Initially, where the horse transitions up to canter on the new circle is not significant. The primary focus is maintaining relaxation, balance, and lightness. The horse can trot as long as needed to produce a good upward transition to canter. The transition sequence only shortens after the changes of gait are fluid.

Temporarily exaggerating the length bend can facilitate the hind-leg lead change. This is done when the horse's stride is suspended in air. The rider helps the horse understand how to change lead by advancing his hips to the inside on the new circle. Take note that the rider always brings the horse to a straight position before advancing the haunch. Never swing the horse directly from one bend to the other. Also note that advancing the haunch to teach lead changes is a short-term departure from the ideal body position. The rider should stop advancing the haunch as soon as the horse recognizes the aids. Once the aids are understood, the absence of bend will facilitate the horse stepping the new lead leg forward smoothly.

While it is advantageous to teach the lead change at *X*, continually practicing in the same place causes the horse to anticipate the change. The horse should instead focus on the rider's aids for direction. Making lead changes along

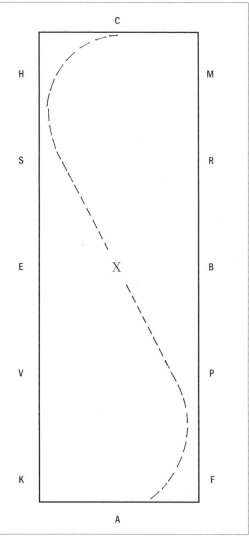

Flying changes. Canter through the corner and down the diagonal line. The rider asks for a flying change as the horse enters the opposite corner.

serpentine or diagonal lines requires the horse to respond to the aids. Mixing in segments of counter-canter stops the horse from being able to predict the exercise, focusing him again on the aids. Good leadership creates scenarios where the horse waits for instructions from the rider.

Expect the horse to be confused by the aids when training begins. He may make arbitrary changes or dismiss the aids altogether. Reprimanding the horse for misreading the aids can be so demoralizing he may refrain from trying. As long as the horse changes lead on both the front and hind legs, it is better to utilize an unintended lead change by immediately applying the aids to reinforce new lead. When the horse changes on only one lead leg, either front or hind, transition to trot without ordeal and start again.

Ideally, flying changes require the horse to listen to the rider's seat bones. The success of this communication is the result of being habitual with the aids and signifies unison between horse and rider. Remember that the rider's overall relaxation allows the horse to distinguish the subtleness of the different aids. When the horse is unable to "read" the rider's seat as an indicator for his position, the rider will have to resort to the additional aids of her leg and/or rein to tell him to change lead.

While the rider strives to make the horse equal on each side, it is almost inevitable that there will be a stronger lead leg. The rider can use this discrepancy to her advantage. By beginning the canter on the weaker side, the horse changes onto his stronger lead. This increases the likelihood for success. Utilizing even a subtle discrepancy will help to build the horse's confidence in this difficult exercise. This should, however, be a teaching tool only. Once the horse recognizes the aids, work the weaker side until it's on par with the stronger.

Preparation for the change and timing of the execution is the key to success. Executing the flying change can be more difficult for the rider than it is for the horse. Learning the exact timing of the aids is complex, and concentration on the horse's footfall is mandatory. There is a tendency for the rider to ask for the change prematurely. If this happens, it is helpful for the rider to step back from the process and trust both the preparation and the horse. Concentrate only on the movement of the horse.

Most horses are capable of a competent single change, though it must be acknowledged that some horses will be very difficult to teach. The reasons can be physical or emotional. Emotional issues usually stem from bad experiences. If a horse has been forced to change leads without proper preparation in the past, the emotional baggage can linger for a long time. Changing a reaction into a response once barriers have been established is challenging. Time and confidence in all other aspects of the training program is the best way to rehabilitate the horse to the idea of flying changes at some point in the future.

The physical conditions that impede the execution of the flying change will likely reside in the horse's hind end. For this reason not all riders may choose to pursue flying changes on their horses. Any such liability will probably have surfaced well before this stage in training; nonetheless, horses differ in their tolerance for stress and pain. Many horses with adverse physical conditions train to lead active and useful lives. What the horse is able to accomplish depends on his ability to maintain relaxation, even through discomfort. When the horse doesn't respond to the aids, the rider should establish what part of the process is misunderstood or can't be done. The questions to ask are:

- Is the horse flexible through the hips?
- Can the horse make upward/downward transitions on the aids?

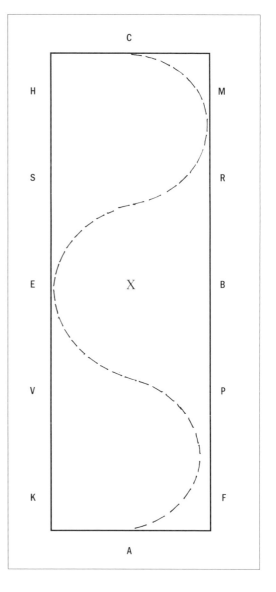

Flying changes. Use three or more serpentine loops to request a change of lead as the horse crosses the center line. Riding some of the loops in counter-canter teaches the horse not to anticipate the rider's directions and to pay strict attention to the aids.

- Can the horse maintain the counter-canter?
- Is the rider relaxed and asking for the change correctly?
- Is the horse relaxed, and if not, why?

Remember, the rider can persist in asking for a flying change without becoming adversarial. However, professional assistance may be needed if the rider can answer all of these questions affirmatively, yet the horse still won't respond.

Patience with the horse and mastery of self pay great rewards to those who pursue lightness. Accomplishing the flying change is confirmation of success. For the academic rider there is no greater honor than to share this accolade with the horse as equal partners.

Horses will naturally respond to lightness once shown the way. While the journey toward lightness as described in this book cannot be achieved by combining different training methods, utilizing the lessons for lightness can heighten the response from any horse ridden under any method.

Lessons in Lightness does not seek to be purist in nature. We salute all riders who either undertake the full vision of lightness or simply choose to introduce the concept of relaxation into their training style.

Thank you for interest in riding in lightness. Your horse will thank you as well, each and every time you ride.

cadence. The embellishment of the natural gait through timing and collection.

flexion. A bending movement around a joint. Flexion decreases the angle between the bones at the joint (the opposite of *extension*).

impulsion. The driving force from the hindquarters that propels the horse forward. It means the horse is pushing more powerfully with his muscles, not simply moving them faster.

lateral flexion. The horse looks slightly to the left or right by flexing the second cervical vertebra (C2) behind the poll.

lateral bend. In cases where the arc of length bend is no longer consistent as, for example, situations in which either the shoulder or the haunch is being emphasized to teach or supple the horse.

length bend. A uniform, balanced arc from the tip of the horse's nose to the tip of his tail along each side of his body. François Robichon de la Guérinière, the French authority on shoulder-in maintained that: "In the shoulder-in the horse learns to bend in its entire length." The arc of length bend conforms to the circumference line of the circle.

longitudinal bend. The roundness over the horse's top line from the tip of his nose to the tip of his tail.

longitudinal flexion. Flexion at the first cervical vertebra (C1) such that the horse's forehead-to-nose profile forms a nearly vertical line.

manège. An area for training horses such as a riding arena. The place where horses are schooled.

savoring the bit. Relaxing the jaw and poll and using the tongue to lift the bit.

self-balance or self-carriage. The horse is carrying the rider's and his own weight in the most efficient way. The weight is balanced beneath the rider's seat. As the horse advances, he is able to carry himself in balance through the various school movements without any support from the rein.

suppling. To increase the flexibility of the horse's joints by stretching and strengthening the muscles around the joints.

suppleness. The ability to flex and extend the muscles and joints without stiffness.

volte (French). A small circle, usually six meters in diameter.

Academic Equitation by General (Albert) DeCarpentry. Reprint. Pomfret, VT: A Trafalgar Square Publication, 2001.

Breaking and Riding by James Fillis. 1902. A facsimile of the first edition, with an introduction by Bill Steinkraus. Guilford, CT: The Lyons Press, forthcoming.

The Complete Training of Horse and Rider by Alois Podhajsky. Reprint. Garden City, NY: Doubleday & Co., Inc., 1967.

Natural Horsemanship by Pat Parrelli. Colorado Springs: Western Horseman Inc., 1993.

Reflections on Equestrian Art by Nuno Oliveira. London: J. A. Allen & Co., 1988.

Yoga for Equestrians by Linda Benedik and Veronica Wirth. North Pomfret, VT: A Trafalgar Square Publication, 2002.

Video

Natural Equine Orthodontics by Spencer LaFlure. Valeo Films Inc., 2003.

MARK RUSSELL, based in eastern Connecticut, is a trainer and farrier who has served New England horse owners for over thirty years. He was inspired to ride in lightness after observing Nuno Oliveira in Portugal. Master Oliveira, like his predecessors in classical riding, believed that enjoyment and success in riding was predicated on first teaching the horses to relax and release tension. Mark has styled a modern teaching system based on the traditional gymnastic routines for releasing the horse's stiffness and tension, thus freeing energy to

travel freely through the horse's body. Processing energy at such a high level allows the horse to become light to the rider's aids and opens the channels of communication between horse and rider.

ANDREA STEELE is a native of England and a lifelong rider. When she first met Mark many years ago, his unique ability to communicate with horses was immediately apparent. She observed the evolution of his system for training and riding in lightness, which inspired her to bring Mark's knowledge and expertise into print. *Lessons in Lightness: The Art of Educating the Horse* is the result.

Andrea lives on a small farm in rural Connecticut with her husband, Willis, and their many animals. She is also an accountant and insurance-industry executive.

Photo: Willis Steele

Mark Russell travels throughout the United States teaching riders and horses how to develop the skills and abilities described in this book. For his clinic schedule or information on private training for horse and/or rider, visit www.markrusselltraining.com.

For ongoing commentary about Mark's vision of lightness, visit www.mouseholefarm.com and join the discussion forum. The blog format of this site encourages riders to share their experiences in the pursuit of lightness, raise questions, and receive comments from Mark Russell and Andrea Steele.

Page numbers for illustrations are in boldface.

longe lines, 63
longe training
assessing left- or right-sidedness,
61–62
free longeing, 70
importance of, 61
learning from observation, 61
providing a good learning
atmosphere, 62
selecting the right equipment, 63
teaching to longe, **64**, 64–65
using the side reins, 65–69, **66**,
67, 68, 69
longe whips, 63
longitudinal bend, **18**, 173
longitudinal flexion, definition
of, 174

M
manège, definition of, 174

N
neck, 72

O
Oliveira, Nuno, 4

P
Phase I long-and-low frame, **22**
Phase I training
overview of, 21–23, **22**
See also canter; circle, beginning
the; frame
Phase II training
overview of, 23–25, **24**
See also frame; lateral work under
saddle
Phase II trot, **24**

Phase III training
overview of, 26, **26**
See also counter-canter; flying
changes

R
rear skeleton, **76**
rein-back
challenge of, 141
in hand, **42**, 42–45, **43, 44**
preparation required for, 139
riding the exercise, 141–46,
142, 145
steps in mastering, 139–41, **140**
yielding the chest, 145
rein position, **99**
relaxation, 2–4, 14–16, **15**, 112
relaxing the jaw
in hand, 33–37, **34, 35,**
36, 37
riding the circle, 96–97
renvers (under saddle), 129–30,
130, 131
rider position
importance of being relaxed,
14, 78–79
key points for improving,
79–80

S
saddles, **84**, 84–85, **85**
savoring the bit, 106, 174
School of Versailles, 2
self-balance, definition of, 174
self-carriage, definition of, 174
short arenas, **11**
shoulder-out (in hand), 50–54, **51,**
52, 53, 54